Equipping the Saints

James Hart Brumm, Editor

The Historical Series of the Reformed Church in America

No. 35

Equipping the Saints
The Synod of New York, 1800-2000

James Hart Brumm, Editor

Wm. B. Eerdmans Publishing Co.
Grand Rapids, Michigan

© 2000 Wm. B. Eerdmans Publishing Co.
255 Jefferson Ave. S.E., Grand Rapids, MI 49503

Printed in the United States of America

04 03 02 01 00   5 4 3 2 1

ISBN 0-8028-4879-6

To
Helen Hertel and all the other saints
who are the Synod of New York,
and
who make it such a wondrous
place for ministry.

The Historical Series of the Reformed Church in America

This series has been inaugurated by the General Synod of the Reformed Church in America, acting through its Commission on History, for the purpose of encouraging historical research and providing a medium wherein this knowledge may be shared with the academic community and with the members of the denomination in order that a knowledge of the past may contribute to right action in the present.

General Editor

The Reverend Donald J. Bruggink, Ph.D.
Western Theological Seminary

Commission on History

Gerald F. De Jong, Ph.D., Orange City, Iowa
Sophie Mathonnet-Vander Well, M.Div., Pella, Iowa
Christopher Moore, New York, New York
Jennifer Reece, M.Div., Princeton, New Jersey
Jeffrey Tyler, Ph.D., Hope College, Holland, Michigan

Contents

The Authors

James Hart Brumm is pastor of the Blooming Grove Reformed Church in Rensselaer, New York, and adjunct assistant professor for RCA studies at New Brunswick Theological Seminary.

Scott Conrad is pastor of the Flatbush Reformed Church in Saugerties, New York.

Herman D. DeJong is pastor of the Steinway Reformed Church in Astoria, Queens, and stated clerk for the Regional Synod of New York.

Micheal Edwards is chaplain at Lincoln Hospital in New York City.

Russell Gasero is the archivist of the Reformed Church in America.

Stephen Hanson is pastor of the Rochester Reformed Church in Accord, New York.

John E. Hiemstra is executive secretary emeritus of the Synod of New York. He currently serves as executive director for the Council of Churches in the City of New York and as co-pastor of the Closter Reformed Church.

Anna Melissa James is a minister on the staff of the Middle Collegiate Church in New York City.

Betty L. King is a certified legal assistant, who serves as archivist and historian for the St. Thomas Reformed Church, Virgin Islands. She was the 1996 Albert A. Smith Fellow in Reformed Church History at New Brunswick Theological Seminary.

Christopher Moore is an educator and historian. He is a member of the great consistory of the Collegiate Church of New York and a member of the RCA Commission on History.

Acknowledgments

If you don't want to be deluged with this sort of thing, keep
your big mouth shut!

> —*Erik Routley,* letter to Howard Hageman
> regarding the latter's appointment to chair
> a committee that would create *Rejoice in the*
> *Lord,* March 21, 1979

This is one of the many pearls of wisdom that can be unearthed
in the Archives of the Reformed Church in America. Some of us,
however, seemingly cannot learn from history...

In the spring of 1998, I mentioned to an RCA history class I was
teaching that the year 2000 would be the bicentennial of New York
Synod's founding, and that it would be an interesting project for
someone to write a history. I'm sure I mentioned this one or two
other times, because, at General Synod the following June, I found
Arthur Hessinger (then president of RSNY) and Donald Bruggink
huddled in a corner of the lunch room. They invited me over and
presented me with the opportunity to edit this volume.

Like most things that happen in the Synod of New York, this
work was both a labor of love and a communal effort. In addition

to the authors who have contributed to this work, there were several people involved in identifying topics to be covered and helping recruit the writers; these included Ella Campbell, Luis Perez, Rodney Koopmans, and the staff at the Collegiate Church Archives. Helen Hertel, Jon Norton, David Maris, and Clara Woodson, my colleagues on the RSNY staff, gave helpful comments and advice, and Helen took time from her other duties to select photographs to use in the book. Members of the Synod Executive Committee were consistently supportive as I gave them regular updates on the progress of the work. Art Hessinger allowed me to devote all my attention to the creative end of this enterprise, while he made sure the necessary funds were in place. Renée House, Marsha Blake, and the staff of Gardner Sage Library at New Brunswick Theological Seminary gave me and other contributors to this book a pleasant and supportive environment in which to do research. Most importantly, my wife, Kathleen, and my son, Christopher, generously donated my time to the synod so that I could complete the work.

Special thanks also need to be extended to Russell Gasero, RCA archivist—who, in addition to preparing the appendices for this book, donated a holiday weekend to typesetting—and to Laurie Baron, who graciously and expertly proofread the copy. Finally, having served as editor for just this one book, I have a profound respect for Don Bruggink and his tireless work editing this Historical Series for three decades. The dedicated work of talented, capable people such as these should make us all proud to be part of the RCA.

Soli Deo Gloria!
James Hart Brumm
Easter, 2000

The Synod of New York Convened
James Hart Brumm

The *Constitution* of the Reformed Church in America (RCA) and its predecessor bodies,[1] going all the way back to the Great Synod of Dort in 1619, provides for regional or particular or provincial synods. These bodies are smaller than the General or National Synod, but larger than the classes.[2] Originally, according to the Articles of Dort and the Explanatory Articles of 1792,[3] which adapted Dort's church order to the new American republic, the particular synods were to be annual bodies, while general synods were to be triennial in the United States.[4]National synods met even less regularly in the Netherlands, where there was none convened from 1619 to 1816.

---

[1] Before 1869, the RCA was known as the Reformed Protestant Dutch Church in North America, the Reformed Dutch Church in North America, or the Reformed Dutch Church in the United States of America, while, in the Netherlands (prior to 1816), the Reformed Church was called the Gereformeerde Kerk.

[2] Article 47 of the Articles of Dort states, "Once every year (unless an extraordinary session shall be judged necessary) two Ministers, and two Elders, delegated from four or more neighbouring Classes, shall meet and shall constitute a particular synod." Cited by Edward Tanjore Corwin, *A Digest of Constitutional and Synodical Legislation of the Reformed Church in America* (New York: Board of Publication of the Reformed Church in America, 1906), lvi.

[3] Also cited by Corwin.

[4] Edward Tanjore Corwin, *Manual of the Reformed Church in America*, 4th ed. (New York: Board of Publication of the Reformed Church in America, 1902), 134.

By Edward Corwin's[5] reasoning, the General Synod of the RCA did not truly exist until the particular synods of New York and Albany were created in 1800. Corwin notes that the Plan of Union which ended the coetus-conferentie schism[6] in 1771 created both a general body and particular bodies in America that corresponded roughly to a particular synod and classes in the Dort Articles. He sees the period from 1771-1800 as a transition, while the American church provided a framework for the three-legged Reformed stool: doctrine (the theological professorate), liturgy (an approved worship order in English and the publication of *Psalms and Hymns* in 1789), and government (the Explanatory Articles).[7]

In 1800, the synod (identified as a General Synod when the synod minutes were first edited in 1859) felt overwhelmed by the annual meeting schedule and the number of theological students to be examined. Thus, the particular synods of Albany and New York were created, and each had their first meetings in autumn of that year.[8] Over the course of the following two centuries, the Synod of New York has welcomed other ethnic groups into the church, challenged the General Synod in its interpretations of church order, and repeatedly led the denomination in being an *ecclesia semper reformanda*. The essays that follow examine the synod from several perspectives.

---

5 The great RCA historian of the late nineteenth and early twentieth century, author of (among other things) *Manual of the Reformed Church in America* and *Digest of Constitutional and Synodical Legislation of the Reformed Church in America*, and editor of *Ecclesiastical Records of the State of New York*.

6 A split in the colonial church over issues of self-government and Americanization. For a full account, see Gerald F. De Jong, *The Dutch Reformed Church in the American Colonies* (Grand Rapids, Mich.: Eerdman's, 1978).

7 Corwin, *Digest,* 485-86. For the "three-legged stool" concept of church order, see Daniel J. Meeter, *Meeting Each Other in Doctrine, Liturgy, and Government* (Grand Rapids, Mich.: Eerdman's , 1992). For background on the development of *Psalms and Hymns of the Reformed Protestant Dutch Church in North America*, see my article "John Henry Livingston: Unlikely Hymnal Pioneer," in *The Hymn*, 48, no. 4 (October, 1997):36-43.

8 *Acts and Proceedings of the General Synod of the Reformed Protestant Dutch Church* (hereafter referred to as *MGS*), 1802 (New York: Board of Publication of the Reformed Protestant Dutch Church, 1859), 301-3.

A particular synod—or regional synod, as these bodies are now called in the RCA—is many things: a collection of congregations, a group of tens of thousands of Christians, a variety of demographic constituencies, and a vendor of ecclesiastical services. As this essay is written in late 1999, New York Synod worships in ten different languages every Sunday. It serves in such diverse areas as the New York, Boston, and Raleigh-Durham, North Carolina, metropolitan areas; the U.S. Virgin Islands; and the Hudson and Delaware River valleys.[9] It includes social justice ministries, new church starts, mentoring programs for new pastors, youth and educational ministries, and after-school and summer programs.[10] This essay, however, will examine the synod primarily through its minutes, as a convocation of classes. In looking at the synod convened, as it were, we will see a body constantly grappling with its identity and its call to ministry in the face of changing demographic realities and in a denomination not entirely comfortable with Dort church order.

The Synod Established

At its meeting in June of 1800, the soon-to-be General Synod adopted a report prepared by John Henry Livingston, James Romeyn, and Solomon Froeligh. All three were ministers; Livingston was the first RCA Professor of Theology, with a growing reputation as "father of the Reformed Church." These three advised that a Particular Synod of Albany be created to encompass the classes of Albany, Rensselaer, Montgomery, and Ulster (or everything north of Rockland and Dutchess counties in New York State) and that a Particular Synod of New York be created to include New York, Poughkeepsie, Paramus, Bergen, and New Brunswick classes (or

---

9   As identified for the 1999 report, "Breakdown of RSNY [Regional Synod of New York] Congregations by Dominant Culture, Size, and Transition within the Synod in the Past Twenty Years," prepared by the RSNY staff, *Minutes of the Regional Synod of New York* (hereafter referred to as *MRSNY*), October, 1999. The worshiping languages of the synod include English, Spanish, Taiwanese, Korean, Japanese, Mandarin, Ghanaian, Indonesian, Thai, and German.

10   See *MRSNY*, May, 1999.

everything else).[11] When the new Particular Synod of New York met in New York City November 19, 1800, Livingston said a prayer formally convening the synod and preached a sermon on Ephesians 4:12, telling the assembled delegates and guests from four of the five classes (Poughkeepsie was unable to send a delegation), that the task of a particular synod was to equip the saints for ministry and to build up the body of Christ.[12] The synod, not surprisingly, elected Livingston its first president and promptly took up the task of establishing itself. Having been given one clear mandate by the General Synod—to examine theological students for licensure and ordination—New York immediately devolved that task to its classes[13] and appointed *deputatis synodi* from among its delegates to observe the examinations on behalf of the synod and report back at the next regular synod meeting. As suggested by the Articles of Dort, a deputy from outside of the examining classis would sit in on each exam, offering advice to the classis and reporting back to the synod on whether or not the examinations were done in order.

While this process was often a rubber stamp, serious attempts were made to maintain the theological integrity of the examinations. In 1866, the Reverend C. L. Wells, in his role as *deputatus synodi*, protested the examination and installation of the Reverend E. S. Fairchild (a congregational minister) by the Classis of North Long Island, insisting that his views on original sin, regeneration, atonement, election, and predestination were contrary to the doctrinal Standards (the Apostles', Nicene, and Athanasian Creeds, the Heidelberg Catechism, the Belgic Confession, and the Canons of the Synod of Dort). The synod censured North Long Island and ordered that Fairchild be re-examined.[14] In several cases, the

---

11 *MGS,* 1800, 301-3.
12 William Henry Steele Demarest, *Address at the One-Hundred Twenty-fifth Anniversary of the Particular Synod of New York* (New Brunswick, N.J.: Archibald Laidlie Memorial Fund, 1925), 16.
13 The classis formally becomes the sole examiner for licensure and ordination with the *Constitution* of 1833. See Corwin, *Digest,* 485.
14 *MPSNY,* 1866, 59.

deputies reported that they were able to relate interesting ideas for examinations to classes they visited, as well as taking pointers home to their own classes.

Without the task of theological examinations before it, the particular synod appointed standing committees on the professorate, missions, prevailing sins, the inspection of minutes from General Synod and Albany Synod, and state of religion reports from its own classes.[15] The synod also appointed delegates to the General Synod as recommended by the various classes.

Of these tasks, it was the annual review of minutes and state of religion reports that would dominate the minutes of New York Synod for its first century and clearly define its character. New York would send to other particular synods and receive from them fraternal delegates, and it would send along, based on a review of particular synod minutes, suggestions for how to deal with issues the sister synods faced. Similar things would happen as each classis related detailed reports of the life of its churches. In its original incarnation, New York Synod seems to have seen itself as an extension of the most collegial aspects of the covenant community.

That collegiality spread to the review of General Synod minutes; New York Synod saw itself on a par with the denominational body, able to respond to it freely and sometimes even to scold it. When the General Synod recommended that baptism only be administered to those children whose parents proved that they possessed faith and piety, New York refused to pass the suggestion on to its classes. Instead, it told the General Synod that its practice was "contrary to the word of God and the standards and usages of the Reformed Dutch Church."[16] After several years without any word from the Netherlands' Synod of North Holland, with whom the churches in America had been communicating since colonial times, the particular synod called on the General Synod to suspend all correspondence with them.[17] New York also advocated for its classes with the

---

15 *MPSNY,* 1800.
16 *MPSNY,* 1816, 6.
17 *MPSNY,* 1820, 6-7.

national body. When the Pompton Reformed Church asked for help with the Reverend Mr. Kanouse, a Presbyterian minister who was interfering in the affairs of the congregation, the synod forwarded a strong complaint against the entire Presbyterian denomination to the General Synod.[18]

The roles were also inverted, with the particular synod calling its classes to their duties on behalf of the General Synod. Even though it appealed to the General Synod to reduce the frequency of statistical reports as early as 1820, saying such reports did not advance the cause of Christ,[19] when the request was not heard, New York dutifully and regularly reminded its churches that the reports had to be filed.

From its earliest days, the synod also had judicial responsibilities. In 1824, it was drawn into the True Dutch Reformed Church schism. At an "Extraordinary Meeting" in November, New York upheld the decision of the General Synod, voting to depose the consistories of Hackensack and Schraalenburgh, whom the Classis of Paramus had refused to remove. The ministers were also deposed, with the pulpits to be filled by the synod, and new consistory elections were to be held "among those who adhere to the rules of the Reformed Dutch Church."[20] By the following May, Paramus reported that the Reverend James Demarest and part of his consistory at Hackensack had been deposed[21] and that a new Schraalenburgh consistory had been organized and was under care of the classis, although a new consistory at Hackensack wouldn't be in place for another year.[22] Most of the old Schraalenburgh consistory, along with its pastor, the Reverend Solomon Froeligh (who had first advocated creation of this synod), had seceded from the denomination in 1822.[23]

---

18 *MPSNY,* 1833, 6.
19 *MPSNY,* 1820, 17.
20 *MPSNY,* November, 1824, "Extraordinary Meeting," 6-7.
21 *MPSNY,* 1825, 11-12.
22 *MPSNY,* 1825, 14.
23 Demarest, 17.

Through all of this, the Synod of New York was growing and changing. In 1812, the General Synod transferred Poughkeepsie Classis to the care of Albany Synod, "in order to even out representation of the Synods at General Synod."[24] The very next year, New York organized the Classis of Long Island with the congregations at Bushwick, Flatbush (Brooklyn), Flatlands, Gravesend, Jamaica, Newtown, New Utrecht, Oyster Bay, Staten Island, and Success.[25] Another year later, Philadelphia Classis was created with the congregations of Philadelphia, Readington, Neshanic, Harlingen, and North and South Hampton.[26] In 1827, the same year in which the General Synod returned Poughkeepsie to New York Synod, New York Classis asked to be divided in half, at Garden Street,[27] and, after a study, the South Classis of New York was created in 1828 out of Courtlandtown, Market Street, Orchard Street, Garden Street, and Tompkinsville.[28] Nine years later, the synod organized the Classis of Passaic (which then included Rockland County in New York State),[29] and asked the General Synod to transfer the new Orange Classis—which was south of Poughkeepsie, after all—to it from Albany.[30]

The 1840s saw the creation of Hudson and Columbia classes[31] and the division of Long Island into North and South classes.[32] In the 1850s, the classes of Westchester[33] and Monmouth[34] were created, and the Classis of Raritan was formed at the request of New

24 *MGS*, 1812, 421.
25 *MPSNY*, 1813, 30-31.
26 *MPSNY*, 1814, 45.
27 *MPSNY*, 1827, 6-7.
28 *MPSNY*, 1828, 7.
29 *MPSNY*, 1837, 26-27.
30 *MPSNY*, 1837, 6.
31 *MPSNY*, 1845, 7-8.
32 *MPSNY*, 1843, 21-22.
33 Tarrytown, Unionville, Greenburgh, Yonkers, Hastings, Bronxville, Greenville, Fordham, and West Farms: *MPSNY*, 1851, 21.
34 First and Second Freehold, Middletown, Middletown Village, Spotswood, Keyport, and Long Branch: *MPSNY*, 1854, 24.

Brunswick Classis.[35] This generation also saw the first noncontiguous classes added to the synod, with Illinois added in 1841 and Wisconsin in 1855.[36] These two both became part of the new Particular Synod of Chicago when it was organized in 1856,[37] the same year that the Classis of Kingston was carved out of Ulster and transferred into New York.[38] This was also the era of New York's only overseas classis, as several members of the Scudder family who were missionaries in India ordained some elders and asked to be organized into Arcot Classis.[39]

By the start of the U.S. Civil War, New York Synod had grown to sixteen classes and 27,900 active adult members.[40] In fact, the synod thought itself too large to do its job well and had already asked the General Synod to create a Synod of New Brunswick, containing Bergen, Passaic, Paramus, New Brunswick, Philadelphia, Illinois, and Monmouth classes, as early as 1854.[41] The denomination

---

35 Raritan included First, Second, and Third Raritan, North Branch, Branchville, Peapack, Bedminster, Lebanon, White House, Easton, Warren, and Plainfield. *MPSNY*, 1859, 6.

36 Demarest, 11.

37 *MGS*, 1856, 90-91.

38 This included the congregations of Bloomingdale, Clove, Dashville Falls, Guilford, Hurley, Second Kingston, Marbletown, New Paltz, North Marbletown, Rochester, Rosendale, and Samsonville. *MPSNY*, 1857, 7-8.

39 *MPSNY*, 1854, 23. The story of this fascinating classis has been told elsewhere by Eugene P. Heideman, but the annual "State of Religion" reports from Arcot give an interesting study in the ups and downs of a nineteenth-century mission. In 1874, Arcot reports the loss of five hundred members due to villages "relapsing into heathenism" (*MPSNY*, 1874, 10) and, in 1876, asks plaintively, "Does our Church wish to have its work here die out?" (*MPSNY*, 1876, 10). But the very next year sees Arcot grow to twenty congregations, a respectable size for any classis (*MPSNY*, 1877, 9), and the next year includes a report that the Christian faith is "strong and growing," despite famine, a cholera epidemic, and only two active missionaries in the entire classis (*MPSNY*, 1878, 8-9). In the years 1882-83, Arcot exults in 718 baptisms and 339 adults received on confession of faith (*MPSNY*, 1882, 8; 1883, 9), and the 1890s see the ordination of Isaac Lazar as the first native-born Christian pastor (*MPSNY*, 1890, 9) and the formation of an active Christian Endeavor youth program (*MPSNY*, 1897, 11).

40 *MPSNY, 1862*, p. 47. These active adults, who would be called "confessing" members now, were then referred to as "communicant" members.

41 *MPSNY*, 1854, 24.

would finally respond to that request fifteen years later, in 1869,[42] by which time New York would have created yet another classis, by forming South Bergen at Bergen's request in 1862.[43]

Yet numerical growth was not the only force stretching the synod. It continued to work at finding its place in the ecclesiastical structure, a task complicated by the General Synod's own journey of self-discovery. While the act which created the general and particular synod structures called for the denominational body to meet triennially, human habits are often much more difficult to change than plans on paper. After meeting annually as a general body and a provisional synod for nearly three decades, the General Synod delegates could not get used to a more relaxed schedule; annual meetings were proposed in 1806,[44] and a yearly meeting schedule was adopted in 1812.[45] This left the larger body time for more work, and soon it was duplicating the work of the particular synods. New York dropped discussions of "prevailing sins" from the agenda in 1815 because "its necessity is superseded, by annual reports of the General Synod on said subject."[46] In 1824, the standing committee on the professorate had also disappeared, again in deference to the work of the General Synod.

Yet the area of finance would provide the first territorial battleground over the prerogatives of General versus particular synods. The first assessments were made by the General Synod in 1850, asking each classis to take a share in cleaning up the church's debts.[47] In 1863, the denomination presented the assessment to the Synod of New York for the first time (and, presumably, to Albany and Chicago as well), asking that it be passed on to the classes. This assessment was to pay for street repairs at Rutgers College.[48] It passed without incident. By the next year, however, when New

42 *MPSNY,* 1870, 61.
43 *MPSNY,* 1862, 48.
44 *MGS,* 1806, 358.
45 *MGS,* 1812, 404, 406.
46 *MPSNY,* 1815, 11.
47 *MGS,* 1850, 105-7.
48 *MPSNY,* 1863, 5.

York Synod received an assessment communication for a total of $2,150, there was extended discussion, and the stated clerk was instructed to communicate to the General Synod treasurer that New York agreed to assess its classes only $1,802.[49] In 1867, the denomination sent along an assessment for $1,600 and insisted that New York classes were in arrears $2,043.73 for "contingent expenses," and that only four of them had paid their share toward the Theological Seminary Endowment Fund. It urged the Synod of New York to take seriously its responsibility for collecting the money, while the synod insisted that it did not know how the arrears amounts ought properly be apportioned, since some classes were exempted (by New York Synod) from the assessment of 1864. Finally, it informed the General Synod that it would happily collect whatever portion of the $1,600 and the arrears amounts were for contingent expenses, but it refused to pass on endowment charges.[50] When North Long Island insisted it had paid its 1864 assessment of $960 but would not pay the 1866 levee "or any further assessments for the above purpose," the particular synod exempted it from "further apportionments for the Theological School."[51]

New York Synod could rightfully argue that it was looking out for the financial interests of its classes in difficult economic times. The questor (predecessor to the modern synod treasurer) had reported in 1865 that eight classes were in arrears in support of the particular synod, and that there was not enough money "to meet the expenses of the present session."[52] The very next year, most classes were caught up with their arrears expenses, but the delinquencies of three classes—Westchester (seven years), Hudson (nine years), and Poughkeepsie (ten years)—had exhausted the synod's funds, and the questor had to pay the cost of the present session ($7.11) out of his own pocket.[53] The next year, a resolution was passed asking

49 *MPSNY,* 1864, 7, 53-54.
50 *MPSNY,* 1867, 5-6, 59-60.
51 *MPSNY,* 1867, 5, 60. The classis was not relieved of General Synod contingent expense charges.
52 *MPSNY,* 1865, 6.
53 *MPSNY,* 1866, 63.

those who were several years delinquent "be earnestly requested to make the necessary payment, as our common duty requires of every Classis."[54]

This had little effect. By 1868, the synod owed its questor $10.65, its clerk $26.00, and it had a $73.23 delinquent bill for the printing of the 1867 minutes. Poughkeepsie claimed that it did not owe any money, since no one had received the bill, and Hudson simply asked to be excused from eight years of its obligations, but the financially strapped synod denied both requests.[55] Finally, in 1869, the entire matter appears to have been resolved, but not before John Brouwer, long-time questor of the synod, died![56]

The first Synod of New York assessments for itself came in 1870, when the synod adopted a formula that called for $3 from "larger" churches, $2 from "smaller" churches, and $1 from "mission" churches.[57] These terms are never defined in the minutes, but everyone seemed to agree upon them, and a century passed before there were any further recorded complaints about the assessments. The assessments were to be paid in September and October, since most of the synod's bills came over the summer. Under this formula, the synod regularly reported a positive bank balance, and almost as regularly saw no need for the assessment at all.[58]

The final discussion of General Synod assessments at the Synod of New York occurred in 1868. That year, the General Synod assessed New York classes $6,150 for contingent and theological seminary expenses, plus $1,321.20 for delinquent contingent expenses and $2,975.10 for delinquencies in the endowment assessment. New York agreed to apportion $550 among its sixteen classes for contingent expenses but refused to pass on the $5,650 in new seminary expenses. It reasoned that nine classes had paid toward the endowment fund and were promised they would not

54 *MPSNY,* 1867, 60.
55 *MPSNY,* 1868, 7-8, 66.
56 *MPSNY,* 1869, 58.
57 *MPSNY,* 1870, 61.
58 The PSNY assessment was suspended for 1873, 1875, 1877, 1889, 1893, 1897, 1903, 1908, 1919, 1923, 1928, 1940, and 1943.

have to pay more, and that the assessment would be an unfair burden on the remaining classes. Nothing was said about the arrears amounts. The synod further overtured the General Synod to take up the entire matter of finances.[59] That was done, and the denomination elected to streamline procedures by billing classes directly for the assessments and leaving particular synods out of it.[60]

Nor was this the only area in which New York Synod staked out its territory and that of its classes against the expanding reach of the General Synod. In deciding a judicial case in 1870, the synod affirmed the following:

> . . . that no resolution, decision, or deliverance of General Synod, can have the force of constitutional laws, to annul or to limit the powers or the prerogatives of the Classes. These powers belong to the Classes—not by derivation from the General Synod, or even from the Constitution— but by original right, as courts of original jurisdiction, and their exercise can be limited only by their own consent, through the provisions of the Constitution which they have mutually adopted. That Constitution defines and limits the powers of the General Synod, and forbids their enlargement, except by an amendment, which must first receive the consent of a majority of the Classes. Whatever force may belong to the deliverances of the General Synod, then, (are) as interpretations of the law; *yet they are not the law!* [sic] For, if they had the force of law, we should have a Constitution like a nose of wax to receive a new twist every year.[61]

That same year, a communication was received from the General Synod suggesting that particular synods spend less time on business the General Synod could do without their input, and instead spend

59 *MPSNY,* 1868, 6, 64-65.
60 *MGS,* 1868, 403-15.
61 *MPSNY,* 1870, 45-46.

more time in devotional exercises. A suggested schedule, including the celebration of the Lord's Supper, accompanied the communication. New York concurred with the idea of spending more time in worship, but thought that it should decide its own schedule and appointed a study committee.[62] The report of that committee, which the synod received in 1871, called for extending the meeting to two days (so that no business would be omitted); adding an evening worship the first day; and suggesting, but not requiring, the occasional celebration of the Lord's Supper, because "the proper observance of the ordinance supposes a previous preparation of mind and heart, which the ordinary routine of business is not particularly calculated to promote."[63] In 1881, the celebration of the Supper would become a regular part of the synod's order of business, continuing even after a vote to stop regular celebrations at meetings in 1883, citing all the reasoning of the 1871 report.[64]

The Synod Defensive

To put some of the synod's concerns from the 1850s to the 1870s into a more general perspective, it is good to remember that the U.S. Civil War was, in large part, fought over the issue of states' rights versus the rights of the national government. While not putting too fine a point on it, one might say that New York was arguing from a states' rights position, in favor of more local control. In the civil arena, of course, the federal government won out. After that conflict, in the 1870s, we find a rise in American patriotism, as the nation celebrated its centennial. The Reformed Church was awash in that same sentiment. It formally dropped the word "Dutch" from its name in 1868, and it celebrated America's birthday with the publication of a collection of essays, *Centennial Discourses of the*

---

62 *MPSNY,* 1870, p. 6.
63 *MPSNY,* 1871, 45. The General Synod of 1873 rebuked PSNY for not following the devotional schedule which the General Synod had laid out for it. *MPSNY,* 1874, 8-9.
64 *MPSNY,* 1883, 52-55.

Reformed (Dutch) Church in America,[65] a volume whose cover is bedecked with U.S. flags and a bald eagle hovering over the RCA crest. Clergy from the Synod of New York distinguished themselves in that book: John A. Todd of Tarrytown contributed, "The Posture of its Ministers and People during the Revolution," explaining that the Dutch colonists were even greater patriots than those of English descent in their war against the British.[66] William H. Gleason of Newburgh added, "The Resemblance of its Polity to that of our own Country," which described our church order as a reflection of the federal system, with the particular synods as subservient states under a supreme General Synod.

This perception was not all that inconsistent with the views of the RCA as a whole. By that time, the General Synod had boards and staff to support, a true denominational bureaucracy. It expected the particular synods to call the attention of all classes to denominational benevolences, and it insisted that classes require their churches to take regular collections for the boards or give reasons not to do so.[67] Hudson Classis responded with a statement, "That the resolution of the General Synod. .requesting that Classis shall require reasons to be given for the failure to take collections for all the boards, is deemed by this Classis to be unconstitutional. Therefore, with great respect, decline to comply with said request."[68] The synod did nothing about this but silently passed it along to General Synod; that body was also, it seems, at a loss for a reply. In 1891, the denomination instructed particular synods to appoint permanent committees on systematic beneficence, and New York agreed,[69] but, in an apparent act of passive aggression, appointed no one at all.

The synod was also coping with growing American civic Protestantism in its own churches, particularly over a repeated

65 (New York: Board of Publication of the Reformed Church in America, 1876).
66 An analysis disputed by John W. Beardslee's essay in *Piety and Patriotism* (Grand Rapids, Mich.: Eerdman's, 1976).
67 *MPSNY*, 1875, 7.
68 *MPSNY*, 1882, 48.
69 *MPSNY*, 1891, 7.

refusal to make use of the Heidelberg Catechism. As early as 1868, Westchester Classis announced that it had appointed a committee to select "an appropriate catechism for use in Sunday-schools and families." The synod's classical minutes committee responded, "'Appropriate' catechisms have long ago been *selected* [sic] by the Reformed Church for the very use referred to in that action."[70] Repeatedly over the next three decades, the synod rebuked classes for not doing anything about the large number of churches who answered "No" to the Constitutional Inquiry question asking whether the Heidelberg was "regularly explained," and it called on classes specifically to investigate all negative responses in 1878.[71]

During this struggle, New York got very little support from the General Synod. An overture went unanswered in 1867, when New York Synod asked for clarification on what the *Constitution* means regarding use of the Heidelberg, "in order that there may be unity, and that in our Reformed Dutch Church the precious truths of the Gospel, in so masterly a manner embodied in, and exposed by, the Heidelberg Catechism, may remain a pure bulwark of preaching, and be the victorious bulwark against the progress of rationalism in the midst of the Church of Christ everywhere."[72] Neither did the General Synod respond to complaint that the denominational instruction in the 1876 *Acts and Proceedings of the General Synod* "to preach [sic] on the Heidelberg Catechism" was inconsistent with Article VII of the *Constitution* (which calls for the Catechism to be "regularly explained") and therefore out of order.[73] Yet the General Synod was quick enough, in that same year, to rebuke New York for only censuring two classes about the use of the Heidelberg in their congregations.

This was not the only front where New York Synod must have felt a lack of denominational support. After its 1866 rebuke of North Long Island for the irregular examination of E. S. Fairchild, the

70 *MPSNY,* 1868, 57.
71 *MPSNY,* 1878, 49.
72 *MPSNY,* 1867, 56.
73 *MPSNY,* 1877, 48.

classis appealed to the General Synod, which reversed the censure and refused to acknowledge New York's protest:

> *Whereas*, the General Synod of the last year, in explaining their reversal of this Synod's action concerning the North Classis of Long Island, use [sic] this language: "Particular Synod was not in a condition to judge the merits of this case, inasmuch as the facts on which the deputatus founded his opinion were not fully before it," and,
>
> *Whereas*, this language does not in our convictions accord with what we know to be truth and fact, and,
>
> *Whereas*, it makes an absolute assertion implicating this Synod as to discretion and fidelity, therefore,
>
> *Resolved*, That this Particular Synod do [sic] now request the General Synod, as an act of justice, so to change its deliverance so as to conform to the facts of the case.[74]

So it wasn't surprising when, in 1871, the synod refused to take any action when *deputatis synodi* Isaac Riley and John McClellan Holmes reported irregular examinations in Westchester and Poughkeepsie, respectively.[75] We might be surprised, however, that upon reading the minutes from New York, the General Synod issued a rebuke for taking no action on these irregular exams![76]

This became a moot point, however, when the *Constitution* of 1874 eliminated the *deputatis synodi* entirely, leaving neither the particular synods nor the General any means to monitor classical examinations.[77] Three years later, it is noted that the denominational body has formally discouraged the continued exchange of fraternal delegates among the particular synods (again wishing to streamline the process and save the synods time and expense). Since the custom had been observed more in the breach than in practice in

---

[74] *MPSNY*, 1867, 8.
[75] *MPSNY*, 1871, 46-48.
[76] *MGS*, 1871, 263.
[77] *MGS*, 1874, 108-109.

recent history, New York reluctantly removed the listing for such delegates from its Formation of Synod.[78] Most of the mechanisms for collegial relationships among classes, particular synods, and the General Synod had now been removed.

The final quarter of the century saw the churches and classes of New York Synod struggling more than at any previous time. Poughkeepsie had many churches that could not abide the denominationally required hymnal, *Hymns of the Church*, and, after being rebuffed by the General Synod, asked the Synod of New York to help it convince the denomination to allow other books to be used. New York Synod thought that the problem was with the tunes and suggested seeking different tunes while using the same book.[79] Poughkeepsie would, ultimately, grow weary of waiting for denominational sanction and approve a different book for use in its congregations.[80]

Other congregations had more serious, or at least more institutionally pressing, concerns. After some struggle, the two classes of New York were merged back together for mutual support.[81] In 1875-1876, benevolent giving in the synod dropped by more than $23,000.[82] New York Classis fretted that its churches were unwilling to spend more time in prayer and mutual support, while Orange noted that its congregations were "brought very low, mourning the absence of God's converting grace."[83] In the 1890s, the synod was concerned with "poor temporal prospects" for the church on St. Thomas,[84] with substantial losses of members in both

---

78 *MPSNY,* 1877, 50. The synod continued to examine the minutes of the other synods and receive communications from them.
79 *MPSNY,* 1876, 46-47.
80 For more on this see my monograph, *Singing the Lord's Song: A History of the English-language Hymnals of the Reformed Church in America* (New Brunswick, N.J.: Historical Society of the Reformed Church in America, 1990).
81 *MPSNY,* 1872, p. 42. *MPSNY,* 1873, pp. 41-42. *MPSNY,* 1875, pp. 6, 47. The North Brooklyn congregation becomes part of South Classis of Long Island.
82 *MPSNY,* 1876, 9. *MPSNY,* 1877, 8.
83 *MPSNY,* 1873, 20-21, 39.
84 *MPSNY,* 1895, 27.

Long Island classes as well as in Kingston,[85] and with its first substantial losses in active adult members. By 1903, the loss of members was so severe that the State of Religion committee wrote:

> We recommend that instead of revising hundreds and thousands of men and women out of the church, the Classes and Consistories institute a search to bring these lost sheep back to the Great Shepherd's fold. Surely it is as important to keep them as it is to win them.[86]

The General Synod continually wanted to "do" something with particular synods during this period. In 1875, it called on New York to be sure to publish all the annual statistical tables—New York pointed out that it already did so.[87] In 1889, the denomination chided New York for not listing separately the donations for "Schemes of the Church," while asking the synod to spend more time discussing evangelism.[88] A year later, all the particular synods were instructed—a forceful word in RCA polity—to record in their State of Religion reports "any figures, facts, queries or suggestions affecting Sunday school work and catechetical instruction, which in their judgment will guide the General Synod's committee."[89]

Yet, even as the denomination tried to find work for the particular synods to do, it wondered about its need of them. The General Synod of 1898 appointed a special committee of three—two of whom, Ashbel G. Vermilye and Edward B. Coe, were PSNY ministers—to study the history of particular synods and determine if they had any future. The committee reported back that particular synods were, in our church order, crucial for "unity of doctrine and discipline, for mutual help and edification," and that the church on every level needed "a better understanding of the place, purpose and '*uses*' [sic] of the Particular Synod" as the best available assembly

85 *MPSNY,* 1896, pp. 8-9.
86 *MPSNY,* 1903, 10.
87 *MPSNY,* 1875, 7.
88 *MPSNY,* 1890, 7-8.
89 *MPSNY,* 1891, 7.

for assisting classes in their work.[90] It is unclear whether the General Synod had fully achieved that better understanding when, the next year, it recommended that particular synods should spend more of their meeting time putting on workshops to present to local congregations the work of the denominational boards, seminaries, and colleges.[91]

More and more, the particular synod was being relegated to the role of sideshow in RCA polity, superintending its classes with limited effect and being treated by the General Synod as an adjunct for denominational promotion. When the Classis of North Long Island, seeing a need for greater attention from pastors, consistories, the Particular Synod, and the denomination for evangelism, overtured New York Synod to hire a superintendent, with primary responsibility for researching church start fields, the synod was forced to decline:

> Such a man, if he could be found, would be entitled to, and should have, a liberal salary, not less certainly than $2,000 or $2,500, and his traveling expenses. But our Synod has no funds, and it has no way of commanding any excess by laying an additional assessment on our churches, many of which already think themselves overtaxed, and are disposed to complain.[92]

Almost another half-century passed before the synod hired the superintendent proposed by North Long Island. But New York did its best to make the most of the hand it was dealt. When the General Synod called its attention "to the propriety of recording the number of collections for the Boards of the Church" in 1883, the synod responded by calling on each of the boards (at the time, Foreign Missions, Domestic Missions, and Education) to send someone to make annual reports, so that the churches and classes would know

---

90 *MGS,* 1899, 496-502.
91 *MGS,* 1900, 840-41.
92 *MPSNY,* 1899, 23-24, 53.

who and what they were supporting.[93] While Education did not respond until 1900, the two mission boards sent a reporter annually, who was granted time on the agenda every year until 1910. The Young Peoples' Society, Disabled Ministers' Fund, and even the magazine *Mission Field* sent representatives from time to time, as well.

New York also continued to advocate for the needs of its classes and congregations as best it could, overturing the General Synod to look into reasons why so many churches lacked ministers when so many ministers were without charge (in 1885, a hundred out of 543 pulpits were vacant, and eighty-two out of 573 clergy were unassigned)[94] and to place its memorial funds in an endowment that could aid "weaker churches."[95]

The synod was also concerned with making its meetings more interesting and useful. Long before the RCA recommendation of 1900, New York added annual presentations of practical and scholarly papers to its agenda.[96] While the delegates soon discovered the need to limit each discourse to twenty minutes, followed by discussion,[97] delegates and guests heard Ferdinand Schenck—who would later become a noted theologian—speak on "The Bible and Materialism," learned about "Evangelistic Services" from William W. Clark, and looked toward "The Sunday-School of the Future," all at no cost to the synod, using home-grown talent. One of the final papers, "Can our Particular Synod be Made Worth While?" was printed in the *Christian Intelligencer*.[98]

There were other positive moves, however small. The synod encouraged several congregations as they started Christian Endeavor

---

93 *MPSNY,* 1883, 48. The Board of Domestic Missions did, at New York's request, appoint William Clark as extension superintendent in 1904, but he didn't even stay in the job long enough to make one report. *MPSNY,* 1904, 6.

94 *MPSNY,* 1886, 60-62.

95 *MPSNY,* 1899, 57.

96 *MPSNY,* 1882, 52.

97 *MPSNY,* 1886, 64.

98 *MPSNY,* 1910, 80. A study or even a collection of these papers would make for a fascinating bit of historical reading.

societies for youth. The Flushing congregation related news of its class to train young people who were preparing to receive Communion and become adult members, and the synod commended the idea to the churches.[99] The New York Federation of Churches and Christian Workers received monetary support and three delegates from the synod.[100] In an ambitious move, the synod cooperated with the Board of Domestic Missions in creating the Classis of Oklahoma in 1906, reaching out to midwestern settlers and Native American Indians.[101]

The general tendency toward retrenchment continued into the new century, however. Classical reports from the 1890s into the 1910s noted the closing of Sunday schools and congregations; the State of Religion report of 1919 asked, "Is the Reformed Church ready for interment?"[102] The next year, out of twenty-six consistories not able to make any report in the whole RCA, fifteen were in New York Synod.[103] Kingston Classis was merged back into Ulster, which was transferred from Albany to New York.[104] After just four years, the synod found itself unable to care for Oklahoma Classis; the "white" congregations were transferred to the care of the Presbyterians, while the Native American missions were placed under the care of the Classis of New York.[105] Members, congregations, and classes were left wondering not only over the future of the Synod of New York, but of the whole Reformed Church in America.

> There has been no widespread awakening in the churches of our Synod; there has been no conspicuous Denominational progress. Our church extension falls far short of our opportunity. There are not being added to the

99 *MPSNY,* 1890, 20.
100 *MPSNY,* 1901, 61-62.
101 *MPSNY,* 1907, 39.
102 *MPSNY,* 1919, p. 11.
103 *MPSNY,* 1920, 9.
104 *MPSNY,* 1923, 10.
105 *MPSNY,* 1911, 75-76.

church those commensurate with our investment as professing Christians. If we were alert we would find multiplied opportunities for making our Church to grow [sic]. Do we consider ourselves sent into the world as Christ was sent? Do we love to be about our Father's business? Is it in any sense true of us, as our Lord said of Sardis, "I know thy works, that thou hast a name that thou livest, and art dead?" Are we more full of play than of prayer? Has the spirit of materialism and extreme modernism filled our souls? Is there any need that our Church needs to be *Reformed* once more and to return in truth to the spirit and practice of the Apostolic Church?[106]

By the end of the 1920s, it was becoming clear that ministry in the Synod of New York was different from every other area of the Reformed Church in America, as the churches here faced "a polyglot population." New York Classis was seen as the most extreme case:

A glance at the reports of the individual churches indicates that this classis presents the most difficult problems in our entire church. With such overwhelming hordes of people of foreign speech and foreign ideals, with very little interest in Protestant Christianity, with an ever fluctuating population, is it a wonder that some ministers report "of 10,000 families surveyed, only 250 are Protestants?" "unsettlement because of removal of home church;" "continued influx of colored people menaces the life of this church;" "neighborhood reconstruction has forced many members to remove to Queens County, pastor recommends transfer of work." Another reads, "a neighborhood ninety per cent Italian, this year will probably decide the problem of continuance or abandonment of this field."[107]

106 *MPSNY,* 1924, 17.
107 *MPSNY,* 1929, 9-15.

The Synod Transformed

Much of this gradual decline continued through the Great Depression and into World War II, although a foreshadowing of a new era was also evident. A committee was appointed in 1932 to study the advisability of reshaping classis boundaries in the Hudson Valley, but it recommended that there was no clear advantage to changing things just yet.[108] The synod's stated clerk was asked to look into reducing the cost of printing the synodical minutes, so that the savings—or a sum no less than $50 per year—could be given to the fund for the Fraternal Relief Union to assist ministers of the synod who were in need.[109] When the Ministerial Pension Fund began to decline, New York overtured the General Synod to create "some kind of a modern, business-like pension plan by which churches and pastors shall make payments to build up a dependable and adequate pension."[110] When the denomination's Contributory Annuity Plan was unveiled, the synod noted it with pleasure, encouraged all its congregations to participate, and asked the General Synod to start the plan as soon as seventy ministers were enrolled, rather than waiting for fifty percent of the congregations.[111]

The president's report in 1941 advocated streamlining the work of the synod and electing the president each year for the following year. A committee was appointed to revise the ways in which the synod did business.[112] War would intervene a few months later, causing all of the synod's activities to be scaled back. But new plans for ministry would begin busting out all over as soon as peace was declared. Two months after V-J Day, all of the synod's ministers and elders and their wives were invited to a conference, during which a special meeting was held. The purpose: reorganize the synod "to make it more meaningful to the life and work of the

108 *MPSNY,* 1932, 32-33. *MPSNY,* 1933, 41.
109 *MPSNY,* 1932, 33.
110 *MPSNY,* 1936, 38.
111 *MPSNY,* 1937, 44.
112 *MPSNY,* 1941, 39-41.

church." In hope of giving the synod responsibility for the "life and work" of its congregations, five permanent committees were created: Judicial Business, Evangelism & Stewardship, Religious Education & Youth Work, Church Extension & Cultivation, and Social Action.[113]

Social action was long a concern of New York Synod. As early as 1816, the synod noted that "considerable attention is paid to the instruction of blacks, small and great, and poor white children, in several churches on the sabbath and other days of the week."[114] The May meeting of 1852 included a public forum on "Collegiate Education."[115] In addition to support of temperance and Sabbath observance movements and very early opposition to state lotteries, the synod took on the legendary Tammany Hall political machine:

> *Resolved*, That we endorse all wise measures looking to the overthrow of the evils which have long prevailed in connection with the municipal government of New York city [sic], and that we invoke the Divine blessing upon such as are engaged in the present religious crusade.[116]

The principal change affected in 1945 was not concern for the welfare of the world in which the synod found itself, but a standing committee to deal with it systematically.

Yet a more profound change came not in the permanent committees, but in the creation of a Synod Executive Committee. The executive committee would carry on the work of New York Synod between its sessions:[117] for 145 years, the synod had only come into existence once a year, sometimes for as little as a day; now it would be a continuing, proactive body. One of the executive committee's first assignments was to create formal rules of order for the synod, requiring two readings at consecutive synod meetings

---

113 *MPSNY*, October, 1945, Special Meeting, 1-3.
114 *MPSNY*, 1816, 6.
115 *MPSNY*, 1852, 32.
116 *MPSNY*, 1892, 54-55.
117 *MPSNY*, October, 1945, 2.

and an annual vote to change them.[118] These would be the first extensive by-laws that the synod would have, marking the first time it thought more than a few policy statements and the denominational *Constitution* were necessary.

The very next year, President Theodore Brinkerhoff—who now had the job of giving the State of Religion report instead of a standing committee—insisted that holding its own statistically was truly a slight decline for the synod. On his recommendation, the synod added its own set of questions to the constitutional inquiries for its consistories, gave the president an expense account to travel among the classes and congregations, and established an ongoing nominating committee to take advantage of available talent.[119]

The transformation was still not complete. In 1947, the new Church Extension & Cultivation committee insisted that "wherever the Reformed Church is a competing church (i.e., wherever other Protestant congregations are in the neighborhood), it is a dying church." It renewed the recommendation, dating back to the last century, that the position of synodical supervisor be created to help classes take advantage of opportunities. This time the recommendation passed, perhaps because of the suggestion that the synod ask the Board of Domestic Missions for a grant to cover half of the anticipated $5,500 budget increase.[120] Even so, when Alvin J. Neevel was introduced as synodical supervisor the next year, an additional assessment of one-quarter of one percent of congregational purposes giving—the first change in the assessment formula since 1870—was required to cover PSNY's share of the supervisor's budget.[121]

Changing finances were among the most immediately tangible realities in this changing synod. By 1954 this body, which had gotten by with $357.56 in the bank in 1943 (the last time the assessment

[118] *MPSNY,* 1946, 25. *MPSNY,* 1947, 9-15.
[119] *MPSNY,* 1946, 12, 14-15.
[120] *MPSNY,* 1947, 18-19.
[121] *MPSNY,* 1948, 9-11.

was suspended), had a budget of $8,900.[122] Another fifty-cent assessment was later added to support church extension and to help establish a revolving building fund.[123] In 1961, a per-member assessment ($0.29) completely supplanted the nine-decades-old formula of $3, $2, or $1 per church,[124] and, by 1973—after a brief and apparently problematic flirtation with the idea of divvying the budget among the classes to raise as they see fit[125]—the per-member assessment became a standard part of synod business. The budget that year was $352,254;[126] it had risen over 984 percent in thirty years, with very little discussion. Rather than wringing its hands over needs it could not meet, as it had for most of its existence, the Synod of New York seems to have been determined to take on the challenge of ministry.

Those challenges were legion. After a year in his job, Alvin Neevel expressed concern over the number of churches closing in Manhattan; this matter would prompt studies and work and the infusion of capital.[127] The needs of an aging population were also demanding the synod's attention,[128] as was the growing challenge of race relations.[129] Neevel pointed out, "Church extension involves more than the establishment of new churches. It also involves the

---

122 *MPSNY,* 1954, 12-14.
123 *MPSNY,* 1956, 28-30.
124 *MPSNY,* 1961, 33.
125 *MPSNY,* 1971, 42-44.
126 *MPSNY,* 1973, 10-11.
127 *MPSNY,* 1949, 23-24. *MPSNY,* 1956, 45. *MPSNY,* 1962, 12. *MPSNY,* 1974, 8.
128 Prompted by a Queens Classis overture, see *MPSNY,* 1965, 35. A permanent committee on the aging was established in 1969, the same year PSNY voted to become a full participant in the United Presbyterian residence in Syosset (*MPSNY,* 1969, 14-15, 17).
129 The synod would encourage all classes to support their ministers in race relations work (*MPSNY,* 1964, 12), struggle to meet the need for African-American and Hispanic pastors (*MPSNY,* 1968, 16), and work to increase the minority representation among Classis leadership (*MPSNY,* 1978, 11). In 1983, the Rev. Earle Hall became the first African-American president of the synod (*MPSNY,* 1983, 10); in 1995, the Rev. John Chang became the first Asian president of New York Synod (*MRSNY,* 1995, 5); and, in 1999, Elder Lula Thomas became its first African-American woman president (*MRSNY,* May, 1999, 5).

retention of churches in a changed community."[130] That same year, the Church Extension & Cultivation Committee set up a system for congregations to receive grant support; within four years, there were twelve congregations receiving a total of $26,640 in assistance.[131]

Recreation and nurture also found a place on the agenda in this era. Since 1949, the synod shared a property at Denton Lake, New York, with the Presbyterians, Baptists, and the Synod of New Jersey as a conference and retreat center. While the property was finally paid for in 1956, the arrangement grew more and more problematic, and New York sold its share in 1959.[132] That same year, the delegates voted to purchase a 456-acre property called Warwick Estates for $235,000[133]

Within a year, when the delegates met at their new conference center for the first time, a Women's Auxiliary had been formed, and the board reported heavy use of the center, including six weeks of summer "youth conferences."[134] A special meeting in October 1960 approved joint ownership of what was being called "Warwick Conference Center" with the Particular Synod of New Jersey,[135] and the Reverend Laverne Vander Hill was introduced as the first full-time executive director of the center in 1962.[136] The ensuing years have seen various financial struggles, the addition of staff, and the near-constant repair, rebuilding, and upgrading of facilities, the most notable being the construction of Camp Warwick on a hill opposite the conference center.[137] In 1998, 1,150 children took part in Camp Warwick, while the camp and conference center were busy throughout the year with various conferences and retreats.[138]

130 *MPSNY,* 1962, 14.
131 *MPSNY,* 1962, 22. *MPSNY,* 1966, 5.
132 *MPSNY,* 1956, 6. *MPSNY,* 1959, 7.
133 *MPSNY,* 1959, 31-32.
134 *MPSNY,* 1960, 35.
135 *MPSNY,* 1961, 7.
136 *MPSNY,* 1962, 8.
137 *MPSNY,* 1984, 13-14.
138 *MRSNY,* May, 1999, 6-8.

As New York Synod met changing ministry challenges, it did its best to prompt the entire Reformed Church to do likewise. Overtures were sent to the General Synod to both protect and expand the pensions of ministers,[139]to oppose apartheid in South Africa,[140] to include particular synod social action chairs in the work of the denominational social action committee,[141] to support conscientious objectors to the Vietnam War,[142] and to oppose the defense policies of the Reagan Administration.[143] When the RCA was slow to respond to the synod's call to admit women to the offices of elder, deacon, and minister of the Word, New York encouraged its classes to admit women to all the offices, no matter what the denomination did.[144]

While all of this was reminiscent of the assertive behavior of the synod about a century earlier, there was an important difference in the character of its work. At the very meeting where Alvin Neevel was introduced as supervisor, he presented an eight-page report, the longest of any at that meeting. The next year, a four-page executive committee report supplemented Neevel's;[145] meanwhile, the reports from classes were reduced to notations of ministerial comings and goings, [146] which were, in turn, dropped in 1979. More

---

[139] *MPSNY, 1948*, p. 32. *MPSNY, 1949*, p. 38.

[140] *MPSNY,* 1952, 52-53.

[141] *MPSNY,* 1958, 32.

[142] *MPSNY,* 1968, 32-33. The synod seemed to be of two minds on this issue: while it strenuously supported conscientious objection and raised profound concern about the war, it supported Queens Classis in denying the Sunnyside church permission to receive draft cards and narrowly voted (20-17) not to receive them itself (*MPSNY,* 1970, 7). When Glenn Pontier was arrested for refusing to submit to the draft, the synod prayed for him, admired him, but, again, narrowly voted (23-17) not to publicly support him (*MPSNY,* 1971, 5-6).

[143] *MPSNY,* 1985, 38-39. The synod was clearly much more of one mind on this.

[144] *MPSNY,* 1970, 11. *MPSNY,* 1971, 12. The Classis of Rockland-Westchester ordained Joyce Stedge as the first female minister of the Word in the RCA in 1973. Joyce Borgman DeVelder, "The Reformed Church in America and the Ordination of Women: Personal Memories," in John W. Coakley and Renée S. House, eds., *Patterns and Portraits: Women in the History of the Reformed Church in America* (Grand Rapids, Mich.: Eerdman's, 1999), 143.

[145] *MPSNY,* 1949, 13-16.

[146] *MPSNY,* 1944, 6-8.

and more, New York Synod was behaving as an entity which related to the classes, rather than being driven by the classes as an extension of them.

Neevel was put to work by the churches of the synod almost immediately. His title of "synod supervisor" was changed to "field secretary" to reflect the term used by other synods.[147] When it came time to renew his contract in 1952, the synod made the position of field secretary a permanent part of the rules of order.[148] In his president's report of 1953, William Heydorn recommended that the field secretary and the stated clerk begin publishing a "news sheet" on a regular basis; New York Synod *News* made its first appearance 1 November, 1953, and continued until 1999.[149] By the time Alvin J. Neevel retired as field secretary in 1964, he had played a role in many of the initiatives listed above, presided over a handful of new church starts on Long Island, and guided the synod through some strategic realignments. Parts of Albany Synod's Greene Classis were added to Ulster, while Hudson Classis became part of the new Columbia Classis in Albany,[150] the congregations of Classis Paramus in Rockland County, New York, joined Westchester to form Rockland-Westchester Classis, and the classes of North and South Long Island became Brooklyn, Queens, and Nassau-Suffolk Classes.[151] New York Classis lost its Appalachian and Native American Indian congregations, which were moved to classes nearer them.[152] Through it all, Neevel was bullish on the synod and saw it as making a positive impact in New York City and its environs.

Albertus Bossenbroeck gave his first report as the new field secretary in 1965 and began to help the synod broaden its

---

147 *MPSNY,* 1951, 6-7.
148 *MPSNY,* 1952, 30-31.
149 *MPSNY,* 1953, 22. At the 1999 annual meeting, the synod voted to discontinue the *News* in favor of quarterly bulletin inserts, which will be seen more widely in congregations (*MRSNY,* 1999, 10).
150 *MPSNY,* 1951, 21-22.
151 *MPSNY,* 1962, 7, 44.
152 *MPSNY,* 1956, 8.

understanding of mission. He asked, "Does it make any less sense to maintain a mission in the Bronx than in Bangalore, in East Harlem than in Ethiopia?"[153] He would later be ahead of his time in affirming, "The local church is where mission takes place."[154] During his tenure, the synod opposed the design of a new chapel at New Brunswick Seminary,[155] and developed an insurance program for its congregations.[156] The churches were still struggling, however, and President Douglas MacDonald recommended adding a second field secretary to free Bossenbroeck to assist local parishes full-time. This plan was rejected, though the synod did ask Bossenbroeck to give greater emphasis to "pastoral" and "human support" work and later reconfigured the field secretary position as an "executive secretary."[157]

It was also during Bossenbroeck's time that the synod's geography took its present form, when the classes of Poughkeepsie and Ulster each voted unanimously to request the merger that created the Classis of the Mid-Hudson.[158] The synod reshaped its committees into Church Life, Mission & Outreach, Church Planning & Development, and Human Support.[159] Under Bossenbroeck's leadership, the Council of Field Secretaries was created in the RCA to facilitate dialogue among the synod staffs. Albertus Bossenbroeck's final report, in 1979, listed thirty-two programs and seventeen training events in the Synod of New York and predicted the growing role of Asian congregations.[160]

Before John E. Hiemstra was contracted as the new executive secretary in 1979, the job description was revised again and the

---

153 *MPSNY,* 1965, 12. Two years later, Bossenbroeck would challenge the RCA, noting that the support of other Protestant denominations for their parishes in New York City was 152 percent of the benevolent giving of those congregations, while the RCA only gave 23.3 percent (*MPSNY,* 1967, 13).
154 *MPSNY,* 1972, 16.
155 *MPSNY,* 1966, 37.
156 *MPSNY,* 1971, 22. *MPSNY,* 1974, 18. *MPSNY,* 1976, 17.
157 *MPSNY,* 1971, 20-21, 37. *MPSNY,* 1973, 23.
158 *MPSNY,* 1966, 10-11.
159 *MPSNY,* 1971, 18-19.
160 *MPSNY,* 1979, 71-73.

decision was made to open a synod office. By June of that year, Hiemstra had established the office at the Second Reformed Church in Tarrytown;[161] within three years, Helen Hertel was the synod's first full-time administrative assistant,[162] and Jane Richardson had been hired as a part-time associate for Christian nurture, becoming full time in 1985.[163] During this time, President Roger Leonard called on the synod to get Hiemstra more staff help, so that pastoral calls could be made regularly on all the ministers, but the synod rejected this notion.[164] John Hiemstra did quite a bit for church extension in the synod, especially in bringing Asian congregations on board; supporting the new church start in Cary, North Carolina; and identifying fields for new churches and redevelopment in each of the seven classes.[165]

The synod continued to adapt to the changing plans of the General Synod, as well. In 1973, the denomination's General Program Council had established regional centers: the Eastern Metropolitan Regional Center (EMRC) was to work directly with the synods of New York and New Jersey and their congregations.[166] Arthur O. Van Eck met regularly with the synod, helping create a symbiotic relationship in programming; it was the closing of the regional centers due to financial difficulties at the denominational level that led PSNY to create the associate for Christian nurture position.[167] By 1984, the General Program Council, looking to continue program work with reduced resources, sent a communication to the synod, insisting, "Our mission is one."[168]

---

161 *MPSNY,* 1978, 29. *MPSNY,* 1980, 13.
162 *MPSNY,* 1982, 15.
163 *MPSNY,* 1982, 11. *MPSNY,* 1985, 11.
164 *MPSNY,* 1982, 43. *MPSNY,* 1983, 7.
165 *MPSNY,* 1985, 48.
166 *MPSNY,* 1973, 42.
167 *MPSNY,* 1982, 10-11.
168 *MPSNY,* 1984, 49-52.

The Synod Ever Being Reformed

The Reverend Charles Stickley, in his 1980 president's report, remarked, "This synod has always been a forward-looking synod that accepts challenge and thrives on the excitement of ministry."[169] When John Hiemstra announced his retirement in 1992, the synod (by then called the Regional Synod of New York) appointed a Futures Committee, which recommended a shift from a programmatic focus to a relational focus: "to be an empowering resource to the classes and congregations." The new executive minister was to spend more time on the road visiting with pastors; the associate for Christian nurture position was eliminated; and three part-time area minister positions were created, to be adjuncts to the executive minister. The new arrangement allowed the synod to be more present among the congregations.[170] Jon N. Norton became the executive minister in 1993; David Maris, Debra Jameson (who was later succeeded by Clara Woodson), and this author became the first three area ministers a year later.

In many ways, the goal of this staff configuration is to make the synod a place where its classes and congregations can relate to and support one another, much as the original plan for the Particular Synod of New York did. Yet there is a staff, and the program committees (Spiritual Life & Education; Mission, Outreach, & Social Concerns; Planning, Development, and Revisioning; and Human Support) and budget still exist, allowing the synod to be proactive in responding to ministry needs. This synod of seven classes and 154 congregations continues to include a variety of cultures and demographics, and it is still seeking new ways to respond to new situations and still striving to live up to the challenge John Henry Livingston laid before it two centuries ago.

"... to equip the saints for the work of ministry, for building up the body of Christ."

—Ephesians 4:2 (NRSV)

[169] *MPSNY,* 1980, 43-44.
[170] *MRSNY,* 1993, 11-24.

The essays that follow examine aspects of the life of New York Synod, including two unique congregations (the Collegiate Church of New York and the Reformed Church on St. Thomas, U.S. Virgin Islands) and the life of churches in the Mid-Hudson Valley, the synod's most rural section. Two essays of personal reflection look at the changes in Queens Classis in the past quarter century and the development of urban ministry in the synod by two ministers who have been part of the work there. Essays on various aspects of Asian congregations, and African-Americans in the RCA explore issues which reach beyond this synod, and yet are integral to its life. In fact, the history of New York Synod and the issues it has faced are a microcosm of the life of the whole denomination. This volume concludes with a historical directory of congregations which have been part of the synod.

At the two-hundred-year mark, the Synod of New York is still a work in progress, as are all the regional synods in the RCA. As the General Synod's task force recommended a century ago, every level of the Reformed Church still needs to learn about the role and the strengths of these middle judicatories, in order that we may make the best use of this unique asset in our relational polity.

2

The Mill to the Millennium
Christopher Moore

> Whether the ensuing year is at the end of the XIX century
> or at the beginning of the XX, it is sure to be a year fraught
> with events of the greatest consequence to us and to our
> children. Let us begin it with our faces toward God.
>
> *West End Collegiate Church Calendar for*
> *the Week beginning December 31, 1899*

Historians tell us that three particularly noteworthy events mark
the dawn of American history —the settlement of Jamestown, the
arrival of the Pilgrims in Massachusetts, and the founding of what
is now New York City. That among these three pioneer communities
only one church—the Collegiate Church of New York—has
survived continuously is an important historical note, remarkable
to persons either oblivious to or obsessed with denominational
history.

New York City, of course, is known for far more today than being
the birthplace of the Reformed Church in America. At 42nd Street
and Times Square, at 11:59:50 p.m. of December 31, 1999, a
countdown of the final seconds to the year 2000 began. It was an
event involving millions of celebrants on Broadway and watched by
more than one billion people via television around the world. It is
reasonable to conclude that absolutely no one weighed the memory

of the city's first Christian worship and found it remotely as significant or meaningful as the evening's countdown to giddy champagne-popping revelry or Y2K blues.

Yet, historically and institutionally, the Collegiate Church remains as watchful of change and the turning of each century as any church, on the island or elsewhere. Arguably, the first American to popularize "1999" as a hallmark date was not the modern-day recording artist formerly known as Prince, but Collegiate clergyman John Henry Livingston, who has left us with millennial predictions almost two centuries beyond his lifetime. In a sermon delivered shortly after the dawn of the nineteenth century, Livingston forecast that by clearly preaching the gospel, the church would play a role in biblical prophesy, with astonishing events happening "immediately before the year 2000, when the Millennium will be fully introduced." Far more out-on-the-limb today than he was two hundred years ago, Livingston predicted no less for 1999 than the fall of "Great Babylon" and the Second Coming of Christ.[1]

In the succession of ministers, Livingston is fourteenth in a line of fifty who have served the ministry of the Collegiate Church. It is established on an island that the ancient Native Americans regarded as holy because of its natural position between fresh water (Hudson River) and salt water (Atlantic Ocean). From Fort Amsterdam to Fort Washington, the church has witnessed war, peace, economic prosperity, phenomenal urban growth, depression, racial conflict, and literally every celebration and disappointment since the first Christian minister arrived nearly four hundred years ago.

A History of the Collegiate Church: 1628-2000

Just south of modern Wall Street, in 1626, a mill was constructed at the northern frontier edge of New Amsterdam, a small village

---

1   *Christian Intelligencer*, August 25, 1838, 17. Several years after his death, the paper published Livingston's 1804 sermon, "The Everlasting Gospel," in a three-part series (Part II, September 1, 1838, p. 19; and Part III, September 8, 1838, p. 25).

located at the southern tip of Manhattan Island. Built to grind bark (used for processing animal hides), the mill served Monday through Saturday as a gathering spot for traders, trappers, and tanners—all key players in the colony's very important fur trading business. On Sundays, the second story loft served as a meeting room for worship services for members and adherents of the Dutch Reformed Church.

Because of a shortage of clergy to serve the American colonies, there was a congregation before there was a minister or a church. Worship services were conducted by *krankenbesuchers*, "comforters of the sick," who were authorized to lead the singing of psalms and to read from an approved book of sermons and prayers. Two years later the first minister (domine) arrived in the colony.

On January 24, 1628, Domine Jonas Michaelius set sail from Holland for New Amsterdam, accompanied by his wife and two daughters. After a long and rough voyage across the Atlantic, the Michaelius family arrived on April 7, 1628. On the first Sunday after his arrival, the domine conducted services in the mill's upper room, administering Communion to a gathering of fifty people—all Dutch and Walloon (Belgian). For the inaugural service, he spoke both Dutch and French, for the French-speaking Walloons.

Unlike the English colonial settlements in Virginia and New England, New Amsterdam when Michaelius arrived was the most multinational port in North America. Dutch, Swedes, Germans, Danes, Portuguese, Spanish, English, and Africans were among the people Michaelius and his family encountered when they arrived in New Amsterdam. Having previously served as chaplain to Dutch outposts in Brazil and West Africa, he may have come well prepared for the diverse climate that later distinguished the growing city and the Collegiate ministry on Manhattan Island.

About Michaelius's wife very little is written and almost nothing is known. Nameless to history, she died shortly after reaching New Amsterdam. A much later generation that initiated a vigorous study of church history lamented knowing so little about the church's "first lady."

> We do not even know her name. The grave in which she lies is unmarked. Somewhere, on the lower end of this island where soaring office buildings stand, Jonas Michaelius and his two little motherless girls, but seven weeks after their arrival, saw her laid to rest in the virgin earth of New Amsterdam and committed her brave spirit with a prayer to God.
>
> *The Rev. Henry E. Cobb (Thirty-third,[2] 1903-1943)[3]*

Succeeded by Everardus Bogardus (Second, 1633-1647), the colony and the church's resilience were tested continuously during and following Michaelius's tenure.

Bogardus, who was raised in an orphanage in Holland, as a youngster had been at the center of a province-wide religious controversy. At fifteen years old, he inexplicably lost both his speech and hearing for several weeks. Claiming to hear messages from God telling him to spread the gospel, he vowed publicly that he would enter the ministry if he would ever regain his lost senses. His mysterious affliction lifted and he later studied to become a clergyman. Like Michaelius, he served in Africa (on the Coast of Guinea in present-day Ghana) before being sent as an ordained minister to North America.[4]

---

2   The ordinal designations refer to each minister's place in the succession of Collegiate pastors.

3   Cobb's remarks plus a comprehensive three-hundred-year review of RCA and Collegiate Church history are contained in Edward R. Romig, ed., *The Tercentennary Year: Reformed Church in America, 1628-1928* (New York: Reformed Church in America, 1928), 70.

4   For good brief studies of Bogardus and other colonial Collegiate ministers, see Gerald F. DeJong, *The Dutch Reformed Church in the American Colonies* (Grand Rapids, Mich.: Eerdman's, 1978), 19-21. Bogardus's life in Holland is extensively and impressively detailed by Willem Frijhoff, "The Healing of a Lay Saint; Evert Willemsz. Bogardus's Conversion Between Personal Achievement and Social Legitimation," *De Halve Maen*, vol. LXVIII (Spring 1995), 1-12.

Called an alcoholic by his critics (who claimed he was even unable to take Communion) Bogardus shepherded the church through much of the next two decades. During the tumultuous period when Director-General Willem Kieft's incessant warfare against the Indians left many men, women, and children dead and the colony terrified, he criticized Kieft's policies regularly from the pulpit.

During Bogardus's term, the colony's first school was established. Known today as the Collegiate School, its origin is sometimes recorded as 1633 (when the first teacher arrived in New Amsterdam) or 1638, when Bogardus appealed to authorities in Holland to send a schoolmaster "to teach and train the youth of both Dutch and blacks in the knowledge of Jesus Christ."[5] One of North America's first clerics to perform and record black baptisms and marriages, documents from his administration remain a valuable source of information about the city's early enslaved and free African-American population.

Upon his arrival in 1633, a wooden church (1633-1642) was constructed to replace the mill for Sunday services. A plain building, with a gambrel roof and no spire, the church faced the East River. Located on a lane that is now Pearl Street, the new church had its detractors, some of whom regarded it more like a barn than a church.

> I replied that . . . there was great need of a church, and that it was a scandal to us when the English passed there, and saw only a mean barn in which we preached; that the first thing which the English in New England built, after their dwellings, was a fine church, and we ought to do so, too.
>
> *Notes of David Pietersz De Vries on a conversation*
> *with Director-General Kieft, 1642*[6]

5 Carlton Mabee, *Black Education in New York State* (Syracuse, N.Y.: Syracuse Univ. Press, 1979), 2. See also DeJong, which includes a thorough review of early church relations with blacks and native Americans, 147-69.
6 J. Franklin Jameson, ed., *Narratives of New Netherland, 1609-1664* (New York: 1909), 326.

Ironically, in 1642, Bogardus and Kieft inadvertently conspired to create the first permanent church. At the wedding festivities of the minister's stepdaughter, the director-general initiated a fund-raising campaign to build a new worship place.

> After the fourth or fifth drink Kieft produced a paper, putting his name to a liberal sum at the head of the list. Each then with a light head, subscribed away at a handsome rate, one competing with the other, and although some heartily repented it when their senses came back, they were obliged nevertheless to pay; nothing could avail against it.
>
> *Notes of David Pietersz De Vries, 1642*[7]

Known as the Church in the Fort, the new stone structure was popularly called the St. Nicholas Church (supposedly because the saint was the figurehead of the Nieu Nederlandt, the ship that brought the first colonists in 1623). The church's slate roof, spire, and weathercock towered over the walls of the fort, so that they were the first sight seen as ships sailed into the harbor. It stood for nearly a hundred years, until it was destroyed by fire in 1741. The era of the St. Nicholas Church, which included the colony's old Dutch Christmas traditions and budding Knickerbocker customs, was later popularized by two American authors: Washington Irving, who grew up in the neighborhood of the old church, and Clement Clark Moore.

The early St. Nicholas Church anchored the local ministry; however, the domine was required to make regular visits to communities outside of New Amsterdam. Until 1652 only one minister served the village and neighboring Brooklyn. That year Domine Samuel Drisius (Fifth, 1652-1673) was hired as the colony's second pastor. Able to preach in Dutch, German, English, and French, Drisius joined Johannes Megapolensis (Fourth, 1649-1670) in serving the local region. During the next decade the two pastors traveled several miles each Sunday ministering to

7   Ibid.

communities in Manhattan's frontier (Stuyvesant's Chapel in the
Bowery), New Haarlem, Staten Island, and Bergen County, New
Jersey. Consequently, as new churches were built and more ministers
were called, the collegiate system developed.

> The pastors of the Collegiate church have always been on
> an equality, excepting the deference which Christian and
> gentlemanly courtesy has yielded to the senior . . . they
> performed in rotation the same services in all the churches.
> They wore, and continue to wear, the Geneva gown and
> bands, in which costume they were accustomed to walk
> from their dwellings to the church on the sabbath-day.
>
> *The Rev. Thomas Edward Vermilye*
> *(Twenty-fifth, 1839-1893)*[8]

In the collegiate system, the consistory of each congregation had
powers of a local nature, but matters affecting the full body were
handled by meetings of the full Collegiate consistory. (In Brooklyn,
the Collegiate Church of Kings County lasted until 1824.)

In 1664, the ruling government changed entirely, as the English
gained complete military control and the colony became New
York—in honor of the new proprietor, James, Duke of York, who
was the brother of Charles II, king of England. Seldom cited, but
perhaps most influential to director-general Peter Stuyvesant's
decision to surrender is the eleventh-hour advice given to Stuyvesant
by Megapolensis and his son Samuel (Sixth, 1664-1669). About to
order gunners at Fort Amsterdam to open fire on the English
vessels, the elder and younger Megapolensis led Stuyvesant away,
prevailing upon him to surrender. Stuyvesant was severely
reprimanded by the West India Company officials in Holland for
giving up without so much as firing a shot. The West India
Company scolded him for "lending an ear to preachers and other

---

8   Vermilye's reminiscences are included in the souvenir publication of the *Quarter
    Millenial Anniversary of the Protestant Reformed Dutch Church,* November 21, 1878, 40.

chicken-hearted persons" and the Collegiate ministers were denounced for their role in the colony's capitulation.

Unfortunately, too, for the ministers, the English conquest meant an end to the salary they received from the West India Company. The ministers were forced to rely upon the English system, which made each parish responsible for paying its minister's salary—a situation that annoyed domine Johannes Megapolensis:

> On Sundays we have many hearers. People crowd into the church, and apparently like the sermon; but most of the listeners are not inclined to contribute to the support and salary of the preacher. They seem to desire, that we should live upon air and not upon produce.[9]

So "unpleasant and degrading" was the collection system that his son Samuel soon returned to Holland.

However dire the minister's circumstances, the colony received far greater economic investment from England than it had from Holland, and the once tiny fur trading village grew rapidly. The English colonies were now linked along the Atlantic coast, and the New York colony was considered prime territory for settlement and development. In 1682, Domine Henricus Selyns (Eighth, 1682-1701) wrote that children in New York City "multiply more rapidly here than anywhere else in the world." By the end of the seventeenth century, the city ranked third in population among the American colonies (behind Philadelphia and Boston).

In May of 1696, King William III of England granted a full charter to Collegiate, establishing the church as the first corporation in colonial North America. With language that anticipated both freedom of religion and separation of church and state, the charter granted "the free exercise and enjoyment...of worshipping God according to the constitutions and directions of the Reformed Church in Holland." As explained by Domine Selyns, the charter's

---

9 Gerald F. DeJong, "Dominie Johannes Megapolensis: Minister of New Netherland," *New York Historical Society Quarterly*, January 1969, 7-47.

most ardent supporter, it provided the church with the much needed ability to manage its own affairs:

> Its contents are in respect to the power of calling one or more ministers; of choosing elders, deacons, chorister, sexton, etc.; and of keeping Dutch-schools ...also, the right to possess a church, a parsonage and other church property as its own, and to hold them in our corporate capacity, without alienation. Also the right to receive legacies of either real or personal property, and other donations, for the benefit of the church, etc. This is a circumstance which promises much advantage to God's church, and quiets the formerly existing uneasiness.[10]

Perhaps best known by the insider Domine Selyns, who had first sought the charter eight years earlier, was that the document protected a valuable land legacy left to the church. Bequeathed by Selyns's wife (Margarette De Riemer, widow of former New York City mayor Cornelius Steenwyck), the land, located in the Bronx, totaled 3,300 acres or about five square miles.[11] Thus the charter had given Collegiate religious freedom and a new sense of security, which set the stage for further expansion. As new areas of the colony were settled, churches were built to serve the new communities.

Toward the end of the century, the St. Nicholas Church was taken over by the British to serve as a military garrison. To replace it, a new church was constructed on Garden Street (1693-1812). Known simply as the Garden Street (later South) Church, it served Collegiate and an Anglican congregation that awaited completion of its newly planned church. On Christmas Day, 1697, the Reverend William Vesey, the first rector of Trinity Church, was inducted at the

10 Edward Tanjore Corwin, ed., *Ecclesiastical Records of the State of New York*, vol. II (Albany, N.Y.: J.B. Lyon, 1916), 1172.
11 William L. Brouwer, ed., *Her Organization and Development: Collegiate Reformed Protestant Dutch Church of the City of New York, 1628-1928* (New York: published by the Consistory of the Collegiate Reformed Dutch Church, 1928), 113.

Garden Street Church. The two congregations shared the church, meeting at different hours, until the following March, when Trinity was completed.

Though friendly ties between Trinity and Collegiate seemed laudable, a rebel leader named Jacob Leisler had emerged as a militant opponent against English rule. Executed after he briefly gained control of the local government, Leisler counted the local domines and Dutch mercantile élite among his enemies, believing they were far too assimilated to English ways.

Gualtherus DuBois (Ninth, 1699-1751) was soon found to be the necessary healer of the ongoing Leisler controversy and other matters which concerned the church into the 1700s, including the new charter and the continued selection of new ministers by the mother church in Holland. On March 29, 1700, the consistory gave its resounding endorsement of this newest colleague as a peacemaker:

> His learning and virtues have justly become an ornament to our church. Through his remarkable zeal, mingled with gentleness, the troublesome disputes which have, through each other's rashness, now for some years past turned our Church topsy-turvy have at least been almost completely extinguished. Every one in the congregation takes the greatest satisfaction in his teaching and deportment.[12]

For over half the eighteenth century, DuBois served as a Collegiate minister. During his term, the first church organ in New York City resonated at the Garden Street Church, and, in 1747, the consistory recommended that ministers limit the sermons to one hour. (They had been known to go on for three.) An hour glass was placed next to the pulpit "so as to remove the complaints about the long sermon, to increase the audiences and hold the people together, and so enlarge the alms and other revenues of the Church."

In the eighteenth century, two more Collegiate churches were built. Just north of where the old village wall (Wall Street) once

12 Brouwer, 17.

stood, the New (later Middle) Church (1729-1844) was constructed on Nassau Street. However, by mid-century, the consistory observed that many young people had become "Americanized," speaking English in more situations than they spoke Dutch. Recognizing that many were becoming Anglicans and Presbyterians, the consistory moved to create a church in which English would be the dominant language.

A short distance away, the North Church (1769-1875) was built on William Street. Constructed after the arrival of the Reverend Archibald Laidlie (Thirteenth, 1764-1779), the church's first English pastor, the North Church was erected exclusively for English services. The first American-born colleague, John Henry Livingston (Fourteenth, 1770-1810), was later called to assist in English preaching. Known as the "Father of the Reformed Church in America," Livingston's leadership helped resolve one of the greatest institutional dilemmas facing any colonial church: its relationship to its dominant European "mother." Livingston adroitly led the denomination's North American churches toward their eventual autonomy.

On July 9, 1776, the great cast iron bell at Middle Church (known as New York City's Liberty Bell) tolled at six o'clock in the evening to announce the signing of the Declaration of Independence in Philadelphia five days earlier. A crowd of soldiers and citizens then marched down Broadway to Bowling Green, where they tore down the statue of King George III. A week later, all of the Episcopal churches were ordered closed. However, in September, British forces drove General Washington's Patriot army up Manhattan Island and out of New York City.

The war had a large impact upon Collegiate, with its three unprotected edifices (the South, Middle, and North churches) in the British-controlled city. The invading army took command of all church property. Middle Church was converted into a riding school for English dragoons by removing the pulpit, gallery, pews, and flooring. The North Church, stripped of its interior, was used as a hospital and prison, and South Church, although left alone initially for use by loyalist church members, was eventually transformed into a storehouse and hospital. Not until after the war's end in 1783 were the churches repaired and restored to their previous condition. On May 1, 1789, the day after George Washington was sworn in as president of the United States, William Linn (Fifteenth, 1785-1805) was appointed the first chaplain of the United States House of Representatives. Both ceremonies were conducted at Federal Hall on Wall Street in New York City, then the capital of the United States.

In 1796, Livingston and John Neilsen Abeel (Seventeenth, 1795-1812) were among the founders and first officers of the New York Missionary Society, an organization of the city's Reformed, Baptist, and Presbyterian churches. Pledged to "propagate the glory of the Gospel of Christ in places which are destitute of it," the society emphasized mission and education, publishing sermons, letters, reports, and magazines about its work.

Livingston's sermon, "The Glory of the Redeemer," preached in 1799, contained these hopeful words:

> It will not be long before the morning will break, and with its rising lustre dispel the shades of night. Another season of refreshing is at hand. Another Pentecost will awaken the churches and amaze the world.[13]

The sermon was printed and circulated widely by the Missionary Society. In the new century, he pronounced his vision of the years 1999 and 2000, giving the church the "short remaining space of 200 years" to complete its missionary task of distributing the gospel worldwide. He delivered his apocalyptic sermon entitled, "The Everlasting Gospel," before the Missionary Society in 1804. Livingston, who was by then professor of theology for the Reformed Protestant Dutch Church (and later president of New Brunswick

---

[13] From *Two Sermons Delivered Before the New-York Missionary Society* (New York: Collins, 1799).

Theological Seminary), ended this address with confidence and expectancy:

> But now a new era is commencing. The close of the last, and the opening of the present century, exhibit strange and astonishing things. Principles and achievements, revolutions and designs, events uncommon and portentous, in rapid succession arrest our attention. Each year, each day, is pregnant with something great, and all human calculations are set at defiance. The infidel, with his impious philosophy, stands aghast, and, destitute of resources, with trembling forebodings, wonders how and where the perplexed scene will end; whilst the Christian, instructed by the word and spirit of the Savior, calmly views the turning of the dreadful wheels, and knows which way they will proceed. Strengthened by divine grace, he stands undaunted in the mighty commotion, and looks up, rejoicing that his prayers are heard, and that his *redemption draweth nigh*.[14]

Nearly two hundred years old and venerated as the city's oldest church, Collegiate became a leader in promoting interest in the city's history. Joining with secular interests, in 1804 William Linn and John Neilsen Abeel met with then mayor (later governor) DeWitt Clinton and nine other influential citizens "and agreed to organize a Society, the principal design of which should be to collect and preserve whatever might relate to the Natural, Civil or Ecclesiastical history of the United States in general, or of the State of New York in particular. It was further agreed that the organization should be called the 'New York Historical Society.'"[15]

On May 8, 1816, in the consistory room of the Garden Street Church, a meeting of invited clergy and laymen discussed the formation of a new organization to advance the cause of Christianity worldwide. The meeting resulted in the formation, a week later, of

14 *Christian Intelligencer*, September 8, 1838, 25.
15 Brouwer, 32.

the American Bible Society. In 1839, a "Jubilee of the American Constitution" was conducted at the Old Middle Dutch church on Nassau Street. Sponsored by the New York Historical Society, John Quincy Adams delivered the oration, "which occupied two hours and was extremely able and appropriate."[16]

As Manhattan's population continued to move uptown, so did the Collegiate Church. A second Middle Collegiate Church (1839-1887) was constructed on Lafayette Place, at the corner of Fourth Street. Another new church was constructed and named the Fifth Avenue and Twenty-ninth Street Church, becoming known later as the Fifth Avenue Collegiate Church, and finally as Marble Collegiate (1854-).

Prior to the Civil War, only one of the Collegiate churches remained in lower Manhattan. Feeling a need to make the church more available to the waves of immigrants coming into the area and the great number of workers who passed by the North Church, a weekly prayer meeting at noon was started in 1857. On September 23, consecrated layman Jeremiah Calvin Lanphier, a merchant known for his gift of prayer and fine singing voice, began a phenomenon which became known as the Fulton Street Prayer Meeting (1857-1960).[17]

The prayer meetings became daily, sometimes drawing crowds of more than six thousand people, and they were often front page news in New York's newspapers. "Will re-open at the close of the prayer meeting" was a common mid-day sign on downtown businesses. Support for the Fulton Street meeting came from within and outside the denomination, as prayer meetings started in other cities. The Fulton Street Prayer Meeting was popularly credited with initiating the national "revival of 1857 and 1858," during which a reported one million Americans converted to Christianity. Twenty years later, New York Presbyterian minister Dr. Thomas D. Anderson commended Collegiate for its innovations

16 Brouwer, 83.
17 "Fulton Street Prayer Meeting—Thirty Third Anniversary," New York *Times*, September 24, 1890, 8.

in spreading the gospel and reaching the seemingly unreachable every weekday.

> It (the Collegiate Church) entered the busy mart, and at the hour of high noon, in the heart of traffic, true to this prophesy, the prayer meeting was enshrined, the Fulton Street Prayer-meeting that has offered up before the Throne the prayers of the world. Ever may this church continue a center of spiritual power, not alone upon this Island, but throughout this nation. Such is the prophesy whose lessons have been so well learned and followed by the Collegiate Church.[18]

On April 12, 1861, the Civil War began, and on April 29 a prayer meeting of all the churches and chapels of the Collegiate Church was held at Marble. A post-war consistory lauded the Reverend Thomas Edward Vermilye (Twenty-fifth, 1839-1893) for his notable stance during the national conflict.

> During the Civil War he was openly and earnestly on the side of those who were fighting for the national existence. In public speech, on suitable occasions, as well as in private, he showed his hatred of slavery and his unfaltering loyalty, and was sometimes stirred by the great issues then at stake to a fervor of eloquence which was unusual with him, and which many of his hearers could never forget.[19]

After the Civil War, the full consistory acted to end the two-century-old collegial system of ministerial rotation. In 1871, the colleagues were permanently assigned to each individual church. Instead of alternating ministers, members of each local consistory would, in rotation, periodically preside at a member church's worship service.

---

[18] *Quarter Millenial Anniversary*, 85.
[19] Brouwer, 47.

In 1874, the Reverend Talbot W. Chambers (Twenty-sixth, 1849-1896), speaking at Marble's twentieth anniversary celebration, looked back fondly on the system which had ended three years earlier:

> For eighteen of the twenty years since this house was dedicated it was occupied by a Collegiate ministry, four pastors officiating in regular alternation; and the present seems a fitting occasion for some remarks upon that system. It was introduced here a century and half ago by our Dutch fathers, who got it from Holland, where it still survives in the city of Amsterdam. The church in Holland doubtless obtained it from the New Testament, where we find our Lord sending out the disciples two by two (Luke, X:1), and afterwards among the apostles, Peter and John, closely associated in Jerusalem and in Samaria (Acts, III, 2: VII, 14). So also, Paul and Barnabas were united for the first foreign mission, and when they separated, each selected a companion, Paul taking Silas, and Barnabas Mark, so that they were still and always collegiate workers—feeling with the wise man that two are better than one and a three-fold cord is not quickly broken.[20]

In 1878, the Collegiate Church celebrated its "Quarter-Millennial Anniversary." The Reverend William Ormiston (Twenty-ninth, 1870-1888) observed the milestone, acknowledging the changes within the church and its membership over a 250-year period.

> ...(T)hough we may differ from our honored ancestors in many things, yet as a church we still retain the same love for the truth of God, and the same zeal for its maintenance, defense and extension; and sustain towards all other evangelical churches the same loving, brotherly regard.

---

[20] Brouwer, 126.

May our precious heritage be the inheritance of our
children.[21]

Meanwhile, another new church was constructed at 48th Street
and Fifth Avenue. Perhaps affected by the city council's decision
after the war to name two uptown avenues in recognition of its early
Dutch history (Amsterdam and St. Nicholas Avenues), the consistory
restored one of its own historic names, calling the new congregation
St. Nicholas Church (1872-1949).

On Tuesday, April 30, 1889—the one-hundredth anniversary of
George Washington's presidential inauguration—religious services
"of praise and thanksgiving" were held throughout the city at nine
o'clock in the morning, the same hour in which religious services
were held a century earlier. The U.S. flag was displayed in front of
all the church buildings under the control of the Collegiate Church,
and bells (including the New York Liberty Bell) were rung at
sunrise, noon, and sunset. For the national Inaugural Centennial
Committee, the Collegiate Church supplied several "relics and
memorials of the period," including the portrait of William Linn,
the first chaplain of the U. S. House of Representatives.[22]

In 1892, two new churches were constructed: the new Middle
Church (1892-) at Second Avenue and Seventh Street, and the West
End Church (1892-) at West End Avenue and Seventy-seventh
Street. To resolve the persistent question of varying Collegiate
church names, the consistory stated formally in April, 1906: "our
churches be hereafter designated as follows: The Middle Collegiate
Church; The Marble Collegiate Church; The Collegiate Church of
St. Nicholas; The West End Collegiate Church."[23] In 1909, a new
church at 181st Street and Fort Washington was given the name,
The Fort Washington Collegiate Church.

Following the Spanish-American War, the Collegiate Church
entered the twentieth century proudly hailing the victory of Theodore

21 *Quarter Millenial Anniversary*, 22.
22 Brouwer, 85-86.
23 Brouwer, 90.

Roosevelt, a former Sunday school student at St. Nicholas Church, as president of the United States. When the nation again went to war, in 1917, the church sent "four ambulances and a kitchen trailer" to France, each bearing a plate inscribed, "The Collegiate Dutch Reformed Church of New York."

At the church's three hundredth anniversary in 1928, a host of commemorative activities, including banquets, boat rides and pageants, lasted from April until June. Women played a significant role in organizing the events. Perhaps they were behind the celebration's extraordinary interest in the previously mentioned unnamed and unknown wife of the church's first pastor, Jonas Michaelius. "Vrouw Michaelius" was honored at a special dinner. The anniversary celebration also included a recognition by the Reverend Edgar F. Romig (Thirty-seventh, 1922-1963) that the church and nation were embracing a much wider variety of ethnic and racial groups than at any time since their foundation.

> Into the making of the word "America" has been poured life-blood from countless and varying human springs. The folk-thought and cultures of a score of lands have entered into the inheritance of the future.[24]

Hard on the heels of the lengthy anniversary celebration in 1928 came the Great Depression, and the Collegiate Church, like almost all people and institutions in the United States, was left reeling. The national economic crisis had adversely affected the church's finances and membership. It was perhaps ironic that, as the church faced its greatest challenge of the twentieth century, Norman Vincent Peale (Fortieth, 1932-1993) accepted a call to minister at the Marble Collegiate Church.

Peale quickly recognized the powerful impact of mass media and, in 1935, launched a weekly radio broadcast, "The Art of Living," which continued for a record-setting fifty-four years. Peale also became copublisher of the world's leading inspirational magazine,

---

[24] Romig, 74.

Guideposts, and cofounder of the first school for pastoral psychology, the Institutes of Religion and Health. One of the century's most influential religious figures, Peale wrote forty-six books, including the all-time inspirational best-seller, *The Power of Positive Thinking.*

> We have been treated, year-in and year-out during the Peale years to a feast at the Marble table, a feast in which the strong meat of God's Word has always been served in ways that lifted our hearts and strengthened our souls.[25]

In 1984, Peale relinquished his post as pastor at Marble. Having ministered through the generations and conflicts of World War II, Korea, and Vietnam, he continued many of his pastoral duties into the early 1990s, giving him by far the longest tenure of any Collegiate minister.

Today, 372 years after the mill church, there are four Collegiate churches. At Marble (Arthur Caliandro, Forty-sixth, 1975-), Middle (Gordon R. Dragt, Forty-ninth, 1985-), West End (Kenneth A. Gorsuch, Forty-fourth, 1973-), and Fort Washington (Charles D. Morris, Fiftieth, 1997-) each congregation, consistory, and pastor continue the church's ministry. In the manner of Collegiate's origin, all are one, yet each is an individual.

Livingston's eternal hope of Christ's return by the year 2000 has not been realized—for many, anticipation of that forever unknown date is an infinitely far greater expectation than was the last midnight of the year. Meanwhile, from Michaelius to Morris, the mission of the Collegiate Church of New York goes forward into another millennium, in part through words taken from the mission statements of the four churches:

> We believe God's gracious Spirit knows no boundaries or barriers and is poured out on all people....
>
> *The Middle Collegiate Church*

---

25 The Collegiate Church *Yearbook,* 1984.

[We are] an inclusive community led by the Spirit of Christ in creating an atmosphere where miracles of change and growth take place....

The Marble Collegiate Church

We enjoy great diversity in age and race and experience and viewpoint, appreciating individual differences as children of one God....

The West End Collegiate Church

[We] welcome, love and nurture all who seek comfort, peace, spiritual guidance, and growth....

The Fort Washington Collegiate Church

3

Historical Overview of the St. Thomas Reformed Church

Betty L. King

A church that has been in existence for more than three hundred years must, of necessity, have a notable history. Even more notable is the fact that, despite disasters both manmade and natural, the St. Thomas Reformed Church (formerly known as the Reformed Dutch Church) never disbanded. Who were these people and the ministers who served them? When and why did they switch from the Dutch Reformed to the Reformed Church in America? What held this congregation together?

The Reverend Edward Tanjore Corwin, in his *Manual of the Reformed Church in America*, puts the founding date as 1660.[1] Research so far has not found any specific references to confirm this date. The St. Thomas *Tidende* printed a "Historical Sketch" in its February 21, 1917, edition that puts the organization date of the church in 1688 by the members of the Dutch West India Company. History books record that the Dutch claimed St. Thomas in 1657. In Corwin's list from the Holland documents[2] is a reference dated April 4, 1644, of a preacher at St. John by the name of John William

---

1   4th ed. (New York: Board of Publication of the Reformed Church in America, 1902), 1040.
2   Edward Tanjore Corwin, *Ecclesiastical Records of the State of New York*, in seven volumes (Albany: published by the state under the supervision of Hugh Hastings, state historian, 1901-1916).

Scotus. According to the various histories of the islands, neither St. John nor St. Thomas was settled at this time. Only St. Croix dates its beginnings under the English and the Dutch in 1625.[3] The Curacao Papers from the New Netherland documents indicate that the Dutch were on St. Croix in 1643 and 1644. With this information it appears that Scotus may have been on St. Croix rather than St. John and therefore that the first Reformed Dutch Church was established there as well. The *Calendar of References to Churches of America*,[4] compiled by Corwin, includes many references to the West Indies in general in the early 1600s. These references were not translated into English, nor were they brought to America.

The church building on St. John was destroyed in a hurricane in 1793 and not rebuilt. A plaque is all that is left of the church.[5] It was transported to the St. Thomas church, where it hangs today. When membership in the church on St. Croix dwindled and the church disbanded in 1792, the communion silver was entrusted to the St. Thomas church. The church building was conveyed to the Lutheran Church in Christiansted. Although occupied by the Lutherans, the building is still known today as the "Dutch Church." The sexton's dwelling belonging to the church was conveyed to the government, and funds derived from the transaction along with funds left in the treasury were to be used for the indigent on St. Croix. In 1883, the elders, deacons and the pastor, Anson Dubois, of the St. Thomas church requested—in a long letter to the Danish government[6]—that the money might better be used as a scholarship for educating young men for the Christian ministry. Preference, of course, was to be given to applicants from St. Croix or another of the Danish Islands. This request was denied. In his reply to the Danish government, Pastor Dubois concluded, "When the way

3 Corwin, *Manual*, 1041.
4 Edward Tanjore Corwin, unpublished manuscript in the collection of Gardner Sage Library, New Brunswick Theological Seminary.
5 Corwin, *Manual*, 1040.
6 Letter from the Rev. Anson Dubois to the Danish government, original archived at the St. Thomas Reformed Church.

opens in providence for the formation of a Reformed Dutch Church in St. Croix we shall feel encouraged to address government a second time in relation to these funds." Any remaining funds have long since been disbursed. The communion silver was returned to St. Croix upon that congregation's reorganization in 1992.

Records do not indicate that the congregation had a building of its own in the beginning, but that it shared a room in Fort Christian with the Lutheran congregation until 1679. Services were held by the Lutherans in the morning and the Dutch Reformed in the afternoon.[7] The Danish government recognized only the Lutheran Church (state church) and the Reformed Dutch Church. This recognition indicates a strong presence of the Dutch population on the island. According to Kay Larsen in her book, *Dansk Vestindien 1666-1917*,[8] on October 16, Pieter Jansen, a Dutchman from Curucao had a fight with Governor Iversen "outside the Reformed Dutch Church." This may have been the building designated on a chart as a Reformed Dutch Church, located in the savanna east of the fort near the seashore. As late as 1850, old tombstones were to be found in the neighborhood.[9]

In 1701, Pierre Labat noted the existence of the church with a regular appointed minister but questioned the existence of a building. The Danish government put out an ordinance in 1707 which forbid any denominations other than the Lutheran and the Dutch to hold worship in buildings consecrated as houses of worship.[10]

Domini Johannes Borm was called in 1736 after the death on St. Thomas of the Reverend Arnoldus Von Drumen. Shortly after the Borms arrived, Mrs. Borm passed away. Pastor Borm caused much controversy during his stay. Oldendorp, in *A Caribbean Mission*, details the problems caused by Borm regarding marriages and

---

7   John P. Knox, *A Historical Account of St. Thomas, W.I.* (New York: Charles Scribner, 1852).
8   (Copenhagen: C.A. Rietzel, 1928).
9   Knox, 36.
10 Knox, 40-41.

baptisms, particularly of the slaves, performed by anyone other than legally ordained ministers as recognized by the local government. This was the period in which the Moravian Church became established, its mission to bring the Christian faith to the slaves.[11]

Borm's pastorate ended upon his death in 1743. Knox noted that he married his "sweetheart" on his deathbed. One hundred forty-three members were received during his time.

The year 1744 began with the arrival of Johannes Paldamus. Church records prior to this date were destroyed in a fire.[12] There were 142 communicants, 89 white and fourteen colored, on St. Thomas.[13] That same year, 39 members were dismissed, most of whom went to St. Croix to help colonize that island. The old church building was abandoned, possibly due to the same fire. A new building was erected at Snegle Gade, No. 7, Queen's Quarter, and Paldamus began a new registry book.

It was during this time that the actions of a certain Peter DeWind are recorded in the *Ecclesiastical Records*. The son of a prominent member of the St. Thomas church, his attempts to perform as an ordained minister in New York churches are well documented in the various letters in the *Acts of the Classis of Amsterdam*. It appears that he did not officially serve the congregations on St. John or St. Thomas, but his zeal took him to Holland and to New York. His mother, Catherine DeWindt, upon her death in 1759, bequeathed Estate Catharineberg to the church.

Shortly after his arrival in 1784, Pastor Francis M. Verboom purchased this estate from the church for $38,000, $30,000 to be used for the ministry of the church and $8,000 for the support of the poor. Despite being described as an immoral person who did much harm to the church, his pastorate lasted 28 years, with 310 new members received. Verboom retired to Holland in 1812 a

---

11 Corwin, *Ecclesiastical Records*.
12 "Historical Sketch" in the St. Thomas *Tidende*, February 21, 1917. Microfilm in the Edith M. Barr Library, St. Thomas, USVI.
13 Knox, 62.

wealthy man, having sold the town lots of Catherineberg for
$100,000.[14]

The 1800s started off with two fires, each of which destroyed the
building. The first fire, in 1804, took the church along with many
other houses. Despite the fact that the building was not insured, the
congregation undertook rebuilding immediately. Fire struck again,
however, destroying this building in 1806. As many of the people
in the congregation suffered losses from these fires so close
together, no attempt was made to rebuild the second time.
Arrangements were made with the Lutheran church to use its
building for services until Verboom left in 1812.[15]

The problems with Verboom's ministry and the loss of the
sanctuary left the congregation scattered and disheartened, but the
members persevered. In 1827, application was made to the Reformed
Dutch Church in the United States for a pastor, and a new era of
growth began with the arrival of Abraham Labagh in 1828. Worship
was held in English for the first time. A Sunday school was begun,
though it did not survive. Labagh was not only well liked by the
congregation but by the whole community. In his thirteen years as
pastor, 155 members were received.

Labagh's ministry "laid the basis, and partially built up a state of
evangelical piety, such as had never before existed in the island."
When a devastating hurricane struck the island in 1837, the only
effect upon the church was a partial loss amounting to $7000, part
of which was attributed to a depreciation of the Smith's Bay Estate
property.[16]

The arrival of Philip M. Brett in 1842 continued this growth.
Knox described him as being a "faithful and energetic minister of
the gospel." Although his stay lasted only three years, it was very
fruitful. The Sunday school, previously abandoned, was reorganized
as a church school serving five hundred children or more. It was not

---

14 Corwin, *Manual*, 1041.
15 Knox, 67.
16 Knox, 71.

only attended by the children of the church, but also by youngsters from the other churches on the island. Worship continued in the Lutheran church, but, with the growth of the congregation, that became an inconvenience, opening the way for a new building.

> We the undersigned, the Pastor and Wardens of the Reformed Dutch Church at St. Thomas, convinced that many of our fellow citizens labor under great inconvenience from the want of sufficient accommodation in the House of God and that many (especially of the poorer classes) are entirely precluded from worshipping their Maker from this same cause. We therefore earnestly desire to remove these difficulties by the erection of a new church edifice.
>
> Finding it impossible however to withdraw the Funds of the church for this purpose, we look to the well known Benevolence of our fellow citizens to aid us in this desirable undertaking. [Note: the following was lined out—and as an inducement to contribute we would offer the lease of a pew free of tax or rent for 10 years to every subscriber of one hundred dollars.][17]

The success of this petition was proved when the cornerstone of the present building was laid September 18, 1844. In the "Specifications of Contract for the Erection of the R. D. Church," the wardens specified the size of the building, materials to be used, paint, windows, and the pews. Article 12 stated, "The ground floor of the Church is to contain one hundred and thirty pews, 90 to hold five persons each and 40 to hold four each. The gallery will contain 38 pews without the organ loft, which is to be partitioned off on both sides and entered by doors." Article 18 specified, "The work must be finished and the building placed at the disposal of the

---

[17] Letter from the consistory of St. Thomas Reformed Church to the General Synod of the Reformed Church in America, June 13, 1843. In the archives of the St. Thomas Reformed Church. This letter was signed by the Rev. Philip M. Brett and all the members of the consistory.

wardens within nine months from the signing of this contract."[18]
Considering the size, materials available, and that it was to include
everything "that is requisite to a Church except the furniture," this
would seem to be an insurmountable task. Nevertheless, the
building was dedicated February 8, 1846.

THE NEW REFORMED DUTCH CHURCH

> The members of the Reformed Dutch Congregation will
> hail with pleasure the announcement that their new place of
> worship will be opened for dedication on the ensuing
> Sabbath. Under the Grace of Almighty God, their exertions
> are about to be crowned with success—the reward of their
> liberality is not far distant. They will once more have a
> temple of their own! where at their own seasons, they can
> offer up their supplications and their thanksgivings, without
> incommoding another congregation (the Lutheran) whose
> consideration and disinterestedness in according to them
> so cheerfully, and for so long a period, the use of their
> church is deserving of highest eulogiums that could be
> pronounced, breathing as it does so clearly the true spirit of
> Christianity, of all pure religion, "do unto others as you
> would be done by.[19]

Brett did not remain to see his mission fulfilled, as he departed in
1845 following the death of his wife. That he earned the respect and
love of the congregation in his short stay was evidenced by the
number of letters he received after his departure and the request
that he print a volume of his sermons[20] at their expense. The

---

18 "Specifications of Contract for the Erection of the R.D. Church," in the archives of
   the St. Thomas Reformed Church.
19 The *Times* of St. Thomas, February 4, 1846. Microfilm at the Enid M. Barr Library, St.
   Thomas, US Virgin Islands.
20 Philip M. Brett, *A Souvenir of a Three Year's Ministry in the Reformed Dutch Church, St.
   Thomas, W.I., 1838* (New York: John A. Gray, 1856).

dedication of the church was performed by the Reverend John P. Knox.

> February 8th 1846, Sabbath. This day our new Church Edifice was dedicated to the Triune God, Father, Son, and Holy Ghost, the Rev. P. Knox [sic], officiating, assisted by Rev. Tolderlund of the Lutheran Church. Sermon from the text Psalm xiviii, 12 & 13 v. Singing by a volunteer choir led by Mr. Brandt. The audience numbered at least 1200 souls, whilst many stood without. The occasion was one of joy and gratitude.[21]

The arrival of John P. Knox as pastor in 1847 continued an era of growth, which culminated in an unprecedented 711 members by the time he departed in 1854. The publication of his book, *A Historical Account of St. Thomas, W. I.*, continues today to be an invaluable history of the island and the "Dutch Church." He also published a small pamphlet entitled, *Statistics of the Reformed Dutch Church, St. Thomas*[22] in 1849, detailing its status. The church had two elders and two deacons, with three officers not in active service and eight "helpers." The Sunday school had twenty-two male teachers and twenty-three female teachers. Scholars numbered 138 boys, 159 girls. School was held from "3 ½ to 5 o'clock P. M." Worship services were held at twelve o'clock noon. He noted a relief society and a missionary society. Pews were rented annually. Destitute persons were provided for as pensioners. There were 331 members in full communion, the earliest communicant listed from 1780 to the latest date of 1848. In his historical account of the island, Knox described the congregation as having very few Dutch members, with the congregation consisting of Presbyterians from Scotland, Ireland, England, and America; German Lutherans; and Roman Catholics.

---

21 St. Thomas *Tidende*, February 21, 1917.
22 (New York: Charles Scribner, 1849).

John P. Knox is also credited with providing encouragement and inspiration for Edward M. Blyden, noted educator and scholar, to pursue an education. Born on St. Thomas in 1832 of slave parents, Blyden was baptized in the Dutch church. Knox's granddaughter, Edith Holden, wrote an exhaustive biography of Blyden, published in 1966.[23]

> This is a true copy from the Consistory of the Reformed Dutch Church, St. Thomas D.W.I extending from 1744 to July 20th 1876.
>
> In 1843 the first Sunday School in St. Thomas was organized in the Reformed Dutch Church by Rev. Mr. Brett, who was the rector at that time.
>
> In 1855 Rev. William O. Allan of Scotland became the Pastor; for 23 years he faithfully laboured here. The Parochial School, which had Teachers from our Island, now had them from Scotland, and became very prosperous, some of our best people having received their education in this School.
>
> In 1870 Mr. Allan organized Bethesda Day School in the lower part of our City for the poorer children, and while the former had been merged into the Government System, the latter is still in existence and is now controlled by the Moravian Denomination.[24]

The following is an excerpt from a letter written by a Lutheran pastor, the Reverend Charles P. Krauth, to a friend. It was supplied by his great-great granddaughter, who was passing through St. Thomas on a cruise in 1998.

> St. Thomas, November 1852
>
> Among all the surprises of your life, I am sure you cannot have had one so great as that I feel, when I tell you that

---

23 Edith Holden, *The Story of Blyden*. In the archives of the Reformed Church in America, New Brunswick, New Jersey.
24 "Historical Sketch," St. Thomas *Tildende*, February 21, 1917.

though I have not been more than twenty-four hours in this city, I am actually a housekeeper and pastor of a church in it—not of a Lutheran church as you might imagine, but of the Dutch Reformed Church under the care of Rev. Dr. Knox. I have commenced at the end—now I will go back to the beginning. Dr. Knox's wife and family have been in the United States since last spring. Mrs. Knox, who had been recently confined, wrote by the steamer of October to her husband that all had gone well, and that she was rapidly returning to health. The steamer Petrel, in which I came yesterday, brought a letter to Dr. Knox telling him that three days subsequent to his wife's letter, after a sudden convulsion, she expired. She left six children, two of them infants: all of them were with her; Dr. Knox of course is obliged to return to the United States, to be gone at least until January-how much longer he knows not. It is highly important his place should be filled. The letters I had brought had made me known to influential men here, and in the evening I was waited on by the officers of the church to beg me to fill his place. So remarkable a call seemed to me to demand a careful consideration, and though our luggage was already on the West End (Santa Cruz) schooner, I had it removed. This morning, feeling that I had all the facts before me, I entered into the arrangement. Part of it is that we are to occupy Dr. Knox's house, one of the most elegant and beautifully situated in the whole place—high, airy, cool, commanding one of the most charming views of sea, city, or mountain that the eye ever fell on. Instead of the confinement of a boarding-house, we have possession of a commodious and elegant mansion, surrounded by the best houses and best society often place. My duties will be to preach once on each Sabbath, and lecture, if I am willing, on Wednesday night. The Dutch Reformed Church is very strong, wealthy, and influential, and the position is very desirable.[25]

25 Manuscript in the archives of the St. Thomas Reformed Church.

In 1866, disaster struck in the form of a cholera epidemic followed by a devastating hurricane, earthquake, and tidal wave. The lucrative trading business the island had enjoyed for so long moved elsewhere. The church entered a period of slow decline, with membership dropping to only 75 in 1897, despite a succession of pastors.

In 1878, a controversy erupted around the sale of the school building behind the church to the government and divided the congregation.

> Mr. Stivens submitted a proposal from the School Board for the purchase of the RDC School Building, to be used as one of the Communal Schools about being established by the Government on the Compulsory System, for the sum of Two Thousand Five Hundred Dollars.
>
> There being a mortgage on the School House and lot of Two Thousand Dollars in favor of the Rev. W. O. Allan, for money advanced by him for the extension and improvement of the School House, it was considered a favorable opportunity to dispose of the property to the Government for the purpose originally intended, therefore after mature deliberation it was RESOLVED to sell the Property to the Government for the use of a Communal School for the sum of $2,500 (Two Thousand Five Hundred Dollars) with the understanding that the Vacant Lot in front of the building, now used as a play ground, shall not be built upon...[26]

It appears that this property was purchased at approximately the same time as the land upon which the present church building stands. Some of the recordings of the properties indicate that a building may have been present, as the above excerpt indicates that the loan from Allen was for renovation. The controversy surrounding the title and use of the land and building continued until recently. Many of the older members still hope for its return to the church.

---

[26] Minutes of the Consistory of the Reformed Dutch Church, February 23, 1878.

In 1899, the Reverend Andrew M. Arcularius began a three-year pastorate. Excerpts of a very lengthy letter written to a friend and printed in the magazine *At Home and Abroad* presented a detailed description of the church and the island.

> The Reformed Church is a good-sized building, and, on a pinch, will hold nearly 900 persons, and possibly more. It has a gallery all around it, the choir being placed in the rear of the church facing the pulpit. The pulpit is mahogany, of which the people are very proud. The church is an easy one in which to speak and I find it very comfortable in that respect. My audience in the morning is excellent, being made up almost entirely of my own people. In the evening the church is crowded, many from the Lutheran and other churches being present, in addition to my own people.

Of the Sunday school, he noted that it was not very large, but prospects were good for it to grow. There were very few books in the Sunday school library. Statistics reported to the South Long Island Classis included an average of a hundred members.

The economic outlook for the island at the turn of the century was poor. Prospects for the sale of the islands to the United States were strong, but no dates had been set. Membership and the financial statistics of the church reflected the sad state of affairs, and the possibility loomed once again that its doors would be closed. Continued aid from the Board of Domestic Missions was needed. In a letter to the Reverend C. J. Scudder[27] dated May 16, 1905, Perlee noted that the sale of the islands would bring an increased presence of the U. S. Navy and prosperity due to the improvement of the harbor facilities.

> ...(A)lthough financially and from a business point of view, our Church does not stand out bright (still in proportion to the much larger congregations here it certainly does compare

---

[27] A minister of South Classis of Long Island, of which St. Thomas was a part.

well in this respect) but in a spiritual point of view I venture to say that our Church is one of such long standing and existence exercises a great influence for good in this community as the Pastors of the other Churches have said, one of whom also said it would be a loss to our Island if our Church were closed.

He noted that, despite its small size, the congregation gave liberally when called upon.

I most earnestly request the Committee and the Classis to give their attention to the spiritual state of our Church on equal terms with the financial condition of our Church, and they will, I have no doubt, see the admirability in behalf of the Master's work here to recommend us to the continued aid of the Board.

In October of 1916, another major hurricane passed directly over St. Thomas, with sustained winds of 125 mph and gusts to 160 mph. Both the parsonage and the church suffered "some" damage. On February 18, 1917, Leslie presided over a memorable service of farewell to the Danish governor, Henri Konow, upon the transfer and sale of the islands to the United States.

Following the purchase of the islands by the United States, the mission board sent one of its secretaries, a Mr. Demarest, to make a study of the conditions of the church and the impact of the purchase on the church. A large number of Navy and Marine personnel were assigned to the island and did not have a chaplain. This presented the church with an opportunity for service to the island. A year later, Bradley Folensbee was assigned as classical missionary to the church by the South Classis of Long Island, and he began his pastorate immediately following graduation from New Brunswick Theological Seminary.

In 1918, the Reverend and Mrs. Bradley Folensbee arrived on St. Thomas. They found the church to be without a missionary society, a midweek prayer meeting, or a young people's society. With much diligence and faith in their mission, the church grew in numbers once again. In an article in the *Mission Field*, Folensbee reported, "[At] last night's service there were 145 present, 30 Marines." The Folensbees left the church in 1923 and returned to the States. They later described their stay in St. Thomas in a letter to Dr. James M. Martin, stated clerk, dated March 8, 1949, as "five of the happiest years of our life...."

In 1938, the Reverend A. Leslie, who had served between 1916 and 1918, returned, but ill health forced him to return home to Canada the next year. At the regular 1941 spring classis session of the South Classis of Long Island, it was reported that the Reverend Bruno Bruns, a missionary of the Foreign Board, was serving the church. He had just returned from Japan, where he had been a missionary for a number of years. As Bruns was a member of the Classis Pleasant Prairie, the church was transferred to Pleasant Prairie in Iowa.[28] In 1948, the church was transferred to the Classis of New York.[29]

In 1943, Bruns made application to the Chaplain Corps of the United States Armed Forces for a commission as chaplain, with the approval of the consistory. The consistory gave him a leave of absence to serve his country, as a contribution to the war effort. Bruns did not return to St. Thomas, however, but continued in his chaplaincy until 1953. Once again, the congregation found itself without a pastor. If not for the dedication of the consistory, the church doors would have definitely and finally closed.

As secretary to this small but loyal body, D. Victor Bornn used his skills as a letter writer to solicit the support and aid of the Board of Domestic Missions as well as that of Bradley Folensbee and the many friends and contacts that he and his brother, Roy Bornn, had made through the years. His efforts were rewarded by the arrival, in 1955, of Charles Ausherman, who served as a summer student

---

[28] Minutes of the meeting of the South Classis of Long Island, April, 1941.
[29] *Acts and Proceedings of the Particular Synod of New York*, May, 1948, 6.

minister that year and returned the following summer as well. A student of the New Brunswick Theological Seminary, Ausherman was well liked by the congregation. The regeneration he sparked continues today. The Reverend Donald Lam arrived in 1958, and the church has not been without a pastor since.

Calvin Hall was dedicated June 9, 1963, as the new Sunday school annex. December of 1970 saw the first edition of the church newsletter, published by the Reverend Herman E. Luben, then the pastor. The Outreach Committee set up an Alien Orientation Program to assist alien construction workers who had been imported from other islands with very little guidance to help them adjust. One of the major problems they faced was how poorly their children were served by the local educational system. In 1972, the Caribbean Summer House Program was instituted to provide a reading program to help these children upgrade their reading skills. This program was the beginning of a very popular summer camp that continues today.

In 1971, the governing body of the church was expanded to include four "councilwomen." These pioneers were Nina Corneiro, Betty Cooper, May Villa, and Regina Bornn. The following year the General Synod opened the offices of elder and deacon to women, so the special designation of "councilwoman" was no longer needed. An after-school program was instituted in 1976, again in response to a need of the children. This program was attended by about twenty-five children from various schools and churches.

Hurricanes once again blazed their paths of destruction across the island, beginning with Hugo in 1989. Hurricane Marilyn devastated St. Thomas in 1995, less than two months after the arrival of a new pastor, Jeffrey Gargano, and his family. Undaunted by the destruction, the congregation held their regular service on the terrace of "Blackbeard's Castle" the following Sunday. Later, the local Hebrew Congregation offered its building on Sunday mornings until the church could be made safe again. What could have been a true disaster was transformed as the St. Thomas Reformed

Church was thrown into the limelight. Volunteers from all parts of the RCA responded to the call for help in rebuilding the church and parsonage. Their presence, particularly in the early months following Marilyn, not only provided the congregation with physical labor for rebuilding; it also brought about a spiritual restoration of their battered lives and renewed their hope.

Although the doors have almost closed on more than one occasion, the RCA, many friends, and former pastors have come to the congregation's rescue. Today the church continues its mission of serving not only the residents of the island but also the "snowbirds" who arrive each winter to enjoy the warmth of the climate as well as the warmth of the people. The Sunday school program, as in earlier times, proves to be popular. A youth program is dedicated to involving young people in the church program. A newly instituted learning center serves students from the church, other churches, and schools with a much needed after-school assistance program, as in earlier times. This was made possible by the acquisition of property across the street from the church in 1997, which provides space for the church office, Sunday school classrooms, and the learning center.

From early in the history of the St. Thomas Reformed Church, education has been one of the major concerns of the congregation and its pastors. In the book, *Night of the Silent Drums*, by Isidor Paiewonsky, there is a reference to an Isack Gronnewald, an old Dutch Reformed minister residing in St. John in 1733, who taught the planter's children to read. He also taught the slaves to read the Bible, despite its being against the law. Volume X, page 27 of the Acts of the Classis of Amsterdam listed him as being of St. Thomas in 1716.[30] His dedication and commitment is representative of all those who have served the St. Thomas Church despite the hardships and personal tragedies so many have endured.

---

[30] Corwin, *Ecclesiastical Records.*

4

The Experience of Black People[1] in the Reformed Church in America

Anna Melissa James

Gayraud S. Wilmore writes, "Without hard empirical data we cannot be sure, but it would appear that Blacks join denominations like the RCA not only because they have moved into White neighborhoods and find these churches readily accessible, but also because they are looking for an alternative to traditional Black religion."[2] While this is certainly true for many in the church today, it clearly does not account for the presence of black people in the RCA from the beginning of its existence on the shores of North America.

When the first Dutch settlers came from the Netherlands to New Amsterdam (now New York City) in 1626, they were accompanied by African slaves. According to Reformed theology, one grew in faith by growing in knowledge about scripture, the catechism,

---

1 The experience of black people in the RCA consists of people from countries all around the world. They are the ones who represent the church today and about whom I speak in this paper. I have used the term "black" to designate the experience of a people in the RCA who are black in color. I have not used the term "Black" to speak about a race of people, since I do not believe such a thing exists. The term "African-American" has been used selectively because it is a nationality and not a color. This was done in order to be inclusive of all people who are black and not necessarily Americans.
2 Black Council of the Reformed Church in America, "Identity Crisis: Blacks in Predominantly White Denominations," lecture prepared for the Second Annual B. Moses James Colloquium on Black Religion by Gayraud S. Wilmore, 1976, 7.

creeds, and confessions. Some early settlers felt responsible for the souls of their slaves and made various attempts to educate them in the Christian faith. In 1638, "Dominie Everardus Bogardus of New Amsterdam requested the authorities in Holland to send a schoolmaster in order 'to teach and train the youth of both Dutch and blacks in the knowledge of Jesus Christ.'"[3] Other church records show a few black people, primarily children, being baptized or married by the church during the late seventeenth to mid-eighteenth century. In spite of the small number of black people documented in church records, they were nevertheless present during that time, since lay and ordained members of the Dutch Reformed Church owned slaves. However, one factor that can account for the discrepancy between the number of black people present and their diminutive representation on the church rolls was the tension between having concern for the salvation of one's slaves and the effect of their church membership upon the slave industry. While there is evidence of evangelism among the slaves, there are also strong indications that this effort was infrequent and rarely supported by a majority of the church. This opinion grew particularly after the fall of New Amsterdam to the English in 1664.

The prevailing question in the midst of this tension was whether it was legal to keep persons in bondage after they were baptized. Clearly there were varying positions taken by many in the Dutch Reformed Church. Surprisingly, one affirmative response was heard from the Reverend Jacobus Elisa Joannes Capitein, who argued in his dissertation at the University in Leiden "that Paul's concept of freedom was spiritual rather than physical."[4] Therefore, with the Bible, he was able to support the legal system of slavery and its scriptural justification. Capitein was "the first black man to be ordained by the Protestant church."[5] He was brought from West

---

3   Gerald DeJong, *The Dutch Reformed Church in the American Colonies* (Grand Rapids, Mich.: Eerdman's, 1978), 163.
4   Noel Leo Erskine, *Black People and The Reformed Church in America* (New York: Reformed Church Press, 1978), 37.
5   Ibid.

Africa to the Netherlands as a slave in the mid 1700s.[6] After being set free by his master he was sent to University. Upon graduation and ordination, Capitein "returned to West Africa where he served as a missionary."[7]

However, by the late 1700s the church began to express desires seeking to clarify the relationship between black people or slaves and full communion with the church. In the Explanatory Articles of the Reformed Church in America's Constitution of 1792, Article 59 states:

> In the Church there is no difference between bond and free, but all are one in Christ. Whenever therefore, slaves or black people shall be baptized or become members in full communion of the Church, they shall be admitted to equal privileges with all other members of the same standing; and their infant children shall be entitled to baptism, and in every respect be treated with the same attention that the children of white or free parents are in the Church. Any Minister who, upon any pretense, shall refuse to admit slaves or their children to the privileges to which they are entitled, shall, upon complaint being exhibited and proved, be severely reprimanded by the Classis to which he belongs.[8]

Although this article was later deleted from the Constitution of 1833, it witnessed to the tension that existed in the church regarding the status of Christian slaves and black people.

In spite of these views, black people continued to be present in the Reformed Church in America even when alternative religious organizations were established. In 1816, the Reverend Richard Allen and the Reverend Absalom Jones established the African

---

6   There is a discrepancy in the date of Capitein's work. Noel Leo Erskine uses 1742 as the year Capitein arrives as a slave in the Netherlands: Erskine, 37. Gerald DeJong uses it as the year of Capitein's work: DeJong, 161.

7   Erskine, 38.

8   Cited by Edward Tanjore Corwin, *Digest of Constitutional and Synodical Legislation of the Reformed Church in America* (New York: Board of Publication of the Reformed Church in America, 1906), lxvi.

Methodist Episcopal Church. This action spurred similar responses by black people in other denominations. In the midst of these transitions, the General Synod of 1816 resolved that "the blacks within the bounds of our congregations be enumerated as part of them, excepting those who belong to other denominations."[9] Although Dr. John Beardslee, III, does not list the names of churches that black people joined at that time, he notes "that black people in large numbers were [indeed] joining other denominations. To this day there are prominent black families in parts of New Jersey who have Dutch names but not Reformed Church membership."[10]

In spite of their new-found opportunities to create self-determining places of worship, some black people stayed and continued to be a presence in the Reformed Church. In 1824, the Classis of New York organized a church specifically for black people. As the result of inner turmoil and confusion, the church was disbanded after six years. Although the RCA's effort was initiated at the request of the "First African Society," it was still a paternalistic act on behalf of the black people of its community. However, in 1876 the Reverend Dr. William L. Johnson began founding mission stations for the newly freed black people in South Carolina. Many have questioned the authenticity of Dr. Johnson's graduate degree from New Brunswick Theological Seminary, since his name does not appear on its rolls. However, "the report of the Board of Domestic Missions to the General Synod of 1898 refers to the Rev. Johnson as a graduate of NBTS."[11] Nevertheless, as a person ordained by the Classis of New York in 1870 and listed as a minister in the Dutch Reformed Protestant Church from 1870-1883 and again from 1901-1913, Johnson clearly considered himself a brother of the church. It is in this vein, I believe, that he persistently sought the support and full inclusion of the newly founded southern mission churches into the

9   John W. Beardslee III, "The RCA and the African-American Community," *Reformed Review*, Winter 1992, 105.
10 Ibid.
11 *Minutes of the General Synod*, June 1898, 452, as quoted by Erskine, 62-63.

RCA. However, while the New York Classis desired the establishment of a church for black people in the early part of the nineteenth century, by Johnson's time its interest had waned considerably. He made several petitions to the New York Classis and pleaded that "if he 'had classical authority and consent he could have organized many missions in destitute regions near Florence, South Carolina....'"[12] The New York Classis responded negatively to Johnson's requests. After several years, he received support from the Philadelphia Classis in 1901. The classis recommended "Grace Church in Orangeburg, South Carolina, to the Board of Mission for a supplementary grant of $400" and installed Johnson as its pastor in 1902. [13]

Prior to Johnson's installation, a committee from the Philadelphia Classis visited the black churches. The committee reported,

> We found the work greater even in extent and importance than had been represented. In addition to his own church at Orangeburg, the Rev. Dr. Johnson has three missions within 7 miles, where religious services are maintained....We have therefore in South Carolina 12 places where the Gospel is being given to colored people and where they are being educated in doctrine and polity of our church.[14]

Despite the success of Johnson and his colleagues, the support of the Reformed Church began to subside by 1904. In 1911, the Classis of Philadelphia announced its desire to cease its relationship with the black churches and asked the synod to aid only one of the churches in the following year. Between 1911 and 1926, all five churches in South Carolina were closed. In spite of the many reasons to account for the Reformed Church's change of heart, this effort set a precedent nonetheless because, for the first time, black ministers were recruited and commissioned by the RCA to do

---

[12] See Johnson file, April 11, 1901 (found in the RCA archives in New Brunswick, New Jersey), as quoted by Erskine, 67.
[13] Erskine, 67.
[14] Erskine, 68.

mission work. Although most of these ministers later transferred to other churches, this experience contributed another chapter to the story of black people in the life and ministry of the Reformed Church in America.

Two other black people also became ministers of the Reformed Church after graduating from New Brunswick Theological Seminary in the late 1800s. While there are no records to substantiate William Johnson's completion of a degree at New Brunswick, John Bergen and Islay Walden are both listed as graduates of the class of 1879.[15] Walden was licensed and ordained by the Classis of New Brunswick in 1879. He served as an evangelist in the Presbyterian Church South in Lassater Mills, North Carolina, until his death in 1884.[16] Bergen was licensed by the Classis of New Brunswick in 1879 and ordained by the same classis in 1880 as a missionary colporteur. "Although he was an African and was blind, yet by simply having his lectures read to him he passed through the seminary in a creditable manner. This reading was done largely by a lady of refinement."[17] He then joined the Southern Presbyterian Church and labored in Columbus, Georgia, from 1880 to 1883. He died in 1893.

In addition to black people entering the RCA as members and seminarians, they also became introduced to the church through the Southern Normal School in Brewton, Alabama. Southern Normal was founded by James A. Dooley in 1911. His goal was to establish a coed boarding school for black children in the South. In 1919 he was able to secure financial support from the RCA through the Board of Domestic Missions and to solicit scholarships for the students from various bodies within the RCA. Southern Normal remained a mission of the RCA until 1993.[18]

15 John Howard Raven, comp., *Biographical Record Theological Seminary New Brunswick, New Jersey 1784-1934* (New Brunswick, N.J.: The Rev. Archibald Laidlie Memorial Fund, 1934), 143-44.

16 Raven, 144.

17 Edward Tanjore Corwin, *Manual of the Reformed Church in America*, 4th ed. (New York: Board of Publication of the Reformed Church in America, 1902), 314-15.

18 The adoption of a new constitution by the Southern Normal School in that year made its relationship to the RCA similar to that of the three denominational colleges. *Acts and Proceedings of the General Synod of the Reformed Church in America, 1993*, 442.

Several graduates of Southern Normal went on to higher education at RCA colleges and seminaries. The Reverend Andrew Branche, a former teacher of music and English at Southern Normal, enrolled at New Brunswick Theological Seminary full time in 1939. "Upon his graduation in 1943 he was ordained to the ministry"[19] and installed as pastor-director of the school. He served in this capacity until is retirement in 1954. The Reverend Samuel Williams was also from Brewton, Alabama. He graduated from Central College in 1948 and Western Theological Seminary in 1951.[20] After his ordination by the Classis of Holland, Williams served as a missionary and teacher at Southern Normal from 1951-1960. He later served in the pastorate at the Pembroke Reformed Church in St. Anne, Illinois (1960-1968), Hope College in Holland, Michigan (1968-1971), and Community Reformed Church in Oakland, California (1971-1990).

During the 1940s and 1950s, more and more "black people were moving into the neighborhoods in which there were Reformed churches and becoming members."[21] Most of these churches had long histories in the denomination and were located in the urban areas of some of our country's largest cities. As time progressed, these churches became multiracial and required the presence of black and Hispanic leaders in order to meet the needs of the congregations. These circumstances presented several black and Hispanic seminarians at New Brunswick with ministry opportunities in a denomination they knew very little about. One such person was the Reverend Dr. Wilbur Thornton Washington. Washington has been serving the RCA since 1954.[22] While still in seminary, he entered the ministry of the RCA as a part-time staff person at the Mott Haven Reformed Church in the Bronx. He has since served

---

19 Reformed Church in America, *Our Church in Action: The Story of the Year 1944*, (New York: Board of Publications of the Reformed Church in America, 1944) 21.
20 Russell L. Gasero, *Historical Directory of the Reformed Church in America 1628-1992*, (Grand Rapids, Mich.: Eerdmans, 1992), 277.
21 Erskine, 78.
22 Gasero, 269.

as pastor of the Pembroke Reformed Church in St. Anne, Illinois (1954-1959), the Community Reformed Church in Oakland, California (1959-1969), and the First Reformed Church of Jamaica in Queens, New York (1985-1994). He has also served on the faculties of Central College and New Brunswick Theological Seminary and as president of the General Synod, 1988-1989.

The changing communities and growing need within the church for black clergy also created opportunities for ministers from other denominations. This was true for the Reverend Dr. James Joshua Thomas who was licensed and ordained in the Presbyterian Church in Jamaica, West Indies, in 1945. From 1953-1961, he served as pastor of the Mott Haven Reformed Church in the Bronx. He later became secretary of the Board of World Missions (1961-1968). Like Washington and Thomas, many clergy from other denominations have found opportunities to contribute to the overall ministry of the RCA.

Often, "important" experiences are the only things that have the ability to change one's attitudes, opinions, and even theology. This was true for the Board of North American Missions, formerly known as the Board of Domestic Missions. The number of black families joining the congregations served by the board steadily increased during the 1950s and 1960s. With the increased exposure to these families, the board's awareness of the conditions under which many people had to live was heightened. The board began to give voice to these ills and to encourage the denomination to address them. In 1957, the General Synod adopted the Credo on Race Relations. Presented by the Christian Action Commission, the credo called the church to repentance and listed concrete ways repentance could be exemplified. It also called for an emphasis on racial inclusiveness in the life of the church; action against segregation in schools, housing, and restrictive covenants; affirmation of racially mixed marriages; and cooperation with other boards and agencies working towards racial justice.

While it was supported by the leaders of the denomination, it was more difficult to implement on a local level. John W. Beardslee has described the resistance many people felt toward endorsing organizations such as the Urban League and the National Association for the Advancement of Colored People.[23] He has also mentioned the protests and aversion many had against the Covenant of Open Occupancy, which was adopted in 1959 and approved by the General Synod in 1961.[24] Members of congregations that accepted the covenant had pledged not to use racial practices in buying or selling their homes. This covenant was of tremendous importance and provided a prophetic voice in the midst of much hysteria at that time. As more African, Hispanic, and Asian people began moving into the cities of the North, communities that had had a long history of being predominantly white were faced with several choices. In order to "protect their property value," they could implement and support policies that would make it difficult for people of other ethnicities and colors to purchase homes in their neighborhoods. Another alternative was for them to welcome the diverse richness other people brought to their community. Or they could flee the city and move to the suburbs.

The popularity of the latter option had a great impact on the work of the Board of Domestic Missions. Despite the efforts of some churches to meet the needs of a changing community, many were dying as a result of their white members leaving in large numbers. The General Synod of 1959 expressed "its moral indignation over the fact that hundreds of people were left without functioning churches in the great cities and instructed the Board of Domestic Mission to 'alert classes to point out the moral dereliction involved in this neglect.'"[25] At the request of the Board of North American Missions, a Commission on Race was formed in 1964 to focus on the issues of civil rights and human relationships. The commission's goal was to "aid, encourage, counsel, and give help to individual members and churches as they sought to witness in the difficult

23 Beardslee, 111.
24 Ibid.
25 Erskine, 79.

areas of Race Relations."[26] It attempted to meet this aim by creating and distributing educational materials that would enable congregations to discuss these issues and move towards implementing the provisions of the credo in practical ways. In an effort to lead the denomination, the Commission on Race made the following recommendations to the General Synod of 1966:

- that the Reformed Church in America declare itself as a church of Christ for all races and nationalities;
- that the pulpits be opened to receive the Word of God and the administration of the sacraments from a 'properly ordained servant of God - red, yellow, brown, black or white';
- that in evangelism every home should be visited on a non-selective basis;
- that family visits with people of other races should be encouraged;
- that the congregation should be organized for community outreach and church committees should press for Equal Housing opportunities, equal job opportunities and better employment, equal educational opportunities, and equal treatment before the courts;
- that the church should purchase services only from agencies or companies that were 'Equal Opportunity Employers';
- that the church pray that the body of Christ may be healed of racial discord; and
- that the church pray for the spirit of oneness in the R.C.A.[27]

While various means to address the problem of race relations were devised on a denominational level, practical work had to

26 Erskine, 81.
27 Report of the Board of North American Mission, June 9-15, 1966, 30, as quoted by Erskine, 83.

continue in order to maintain and develop the churches that were struggling to survive in the urban areas. The implementation of an intern program between RCA seminarians and the Board of Domestic Missions was one effort of the church to meet this need. The intern program recruited second-year seminarians who were willing to take a year off and provide churches with support. In return the students gained invaluable experiences in ministry. The Reverend Dr. Norman Kansfield, president of New Brunswick Theological Seminary, described this program as a life-changing experience for most of the seminarians that participated.[28] Their new-found perspective of the city, its people, and their conditions became a lens through which they read the gospel anew. Kansfield described most of seminarians as ministers who now possess a strong sense of urgency and impatience when confronted with the slow pace of change. He said what changed them most however, was their experience with the people. The spirituality, culture, worldview, and traditions people of African descent brought with them to the RCA, created invaluable experiences for the seminarians who participated in that program.

One of the churches that benefited from the efforts of the Board of Domestic Missions and their internship program was the New Lots Community Church, where elder Sara Smith is a longstanding member. Elder Smith was raised in an African Methodist Episcopal Church in Pennsylvania. After moving to Brooklyn's East New York community, she joined the New Lots Reformed Church in the early 1960s. She says one of the reasons she chose to attend New Lots was because of its style of worship. Unlike traditional black churches, New Lots' worship services were led in a timely fashion. After church, there was always plenty of time for her and her family to go on outings and enjoy the rest of the day. Smith said she appreciated the polity of the church and enjoyed the sermons and the warmth of the congregation. She particularly remembers the sermons that the Reverend Malcolm Evans preached regarding the

28 Interview with Dr. Norman J. Kansfield, October 21, 1999.

tumultuous 1960s and the call for social justice. He constantly encouraged members to live their faith and get involved.[29]

New Lots was one of the churches that came close to dying after its members began moving away due to an influx of Jewish people.[30] In 1947, New Lots became a project of the Board of Domestic Missions. Ann Forester was sent to begin working with New Lots by developing a Sunday school. By 1951, the Sunday school had seventy-one children enrolled and was staffed by a white person and a black seminarian. By the early 1960s, New Lots was a multiracial congregation. Like most of the churches that would later become predominantly black or Hispanic, New Lots was perceived as a mission station by the larger church. In addition to grants the congregation received from the classis and the Board of Domestic Missions, the pastor's home church in the Midwest was often one of its major funding sources. Smith says that, although there was little involvement by the members on a denominational level, there was always some resentment over being perceived as an "object of mission" by the larger church.

This resentment later nourished the goal of self-reliance among black congregations, particularly after the establishment of the Black Council in 1969. Smith, one of the first council members, says that her pastor at that time, who was white, encouraged her to be the church's delegate at the first Black Caucus. Not all the churches with black memberships were so encouraging. In some churches, the pastor and/or consistory discouraged involvement because the council was perceived as divisive and exclusionary, promoting separation rather than unity.

Nevertheless, thirty delegates gathered at the Hotel Taft in New York City August 15-16, 1969.[31] Several decisions were made at this first meeting. First, delegates agreed to call themselves the Black Council. Second, they appointed a committee to determine what should be done with the $100,000 they had received from the

29 Interview with Sara Smith, November 2, 1999.
30 Board of Domestic Mission Report, June 1950, 21, as quoted by Erskine, 78.
31 Erskine, 93.

General Synod. The money was later declined, in light of their desire to be an agent of reconciliation rather than a funding agency.

Smith said several things happened to black people in the RCA after the formation of the Black Council. For the first time, many became aware of the true number of black people that were present in the denomination. This was a surprise for many and an encouragement for all. In light of the information and mutual support black people received from the caucus, outreach to other black members throughout the denomination was a primary focus. For the first time, black people no longer saw themselves simply as pew dwellers, but as members of a larger body called the Reformed Church in America.

Smith said their outreach effort was not an easy task. The Reverend Dr. M. William Howard, the first executive director of the African-American Council (formerly the Black Council), often received negative responses to the notices he sent out to the churches. This occurred primarily where the pastor or consistory did not support the freedom movement. But the council persisted in its efforts, since the churches often became involved once their pastors moved to other pulpits or the number of black people on the consistories increased.

Another benefit was the increased presence of black people on the denominational level. Smith said prior to 1968, there were very few black people involved beyond the congregational or classis level. However, by the second caucus in 1970, elders David Beale and Nida Thomas were appointed to the General Program Council, and the Reverend B. Moses James was appointed to the executive committee of the General Synod.[32] According to Smith, the presence of black people on the denominational level has not only been of benefit to those serving but, by their participation, the sensitivity of many people has been raised, especially as it relates to racism. She also believes it helped the denomination to support the model of inclusivity when it designed the structure of the General

---

[32] Erskine, 97.

Synod Council with close attention to the gender and racial balance.[33]

In a lecture of the Black Council, Dr. Lawrence N. Jones stated,

> since the mid-sixties, Black Christians who are members of predominantly white denominations have been vigorously engaged in efforts to humanize ecclesiastical structures and to transform the consciousness of churches....The enormous effort exerted to achieve justice within the majority Christian bodies has drained off energy that might properly have been expended in enhancing and strengthening the life of the minority communities and congregations.[34]

The African-American Council took this to heart in its formative years. In an effort to work towards reconciliation, the council formulated two primary goals: to develop leaders and to encourage self-reliance among its churches. As Dr. Jones furthered stated,

> Many of [the black] congregations began as mission stations or colonies of the majority denominations, and many continue in this colonial status. Churches must move to self-sufficiency because whoever controls the purse-strings can determine the policy or even the life of a given group. It is difficult to demand justice from someone who is enabling one to stay alive.[35]

In this mindset, the council led workshops designed to teach people about the role of elders and deacons, the polity of the RCA, the *Book of Church Order*, and how to run meetings. It also encouraged churches to take steps toward ending their "mission station"

---

[33] Smith interview.

[34] Black Council of the Reformed Church in America, "An Agenda for a Black Congregation in a Majority White Denomination," lecture prepared for the Sixth Annual B. Moses James Colloquium on Black Religion by Dr. Lawrence N. Jones, 1980, 13.

[35] Jones, 18.

personas and becoming self-reliant congregations. Workshops on financial planning, budgeting, stewardship, and grant proposal writing were offered in order to enable congregations to reduce their dependency on church grants.

The council's effort bore much fruit over the years. Today there are people of African descent serving on the General Synod Council, the boards of both RCA seminaries, the Board of Pensions, the commissions on Christian Unity, Nominations, History, Christian Action, Race and Ethnicity, and Theology, the Commission for Women, and the World Alliance of Reformed Churches. There are also a number of African-American people raised in the RCA and currently serving as pastors or attending seminary. Several of the churches with predominantly black congregations are thriving and have been financially self-reliant for many years. Yet these gains have not come without hardship and turmoil.

By the early 1970s, many of the predominantly black congregations began to recruit black ministers. Smith said that, at New Lots, the Reverend Donald Pangburn worked for two years to prepare the congregation for this transition. Even though congregations felt great anticipation and excitement, this transition was frequently filled with confusion, disappointment, and turmoil. In the end, many congregations were left barely surviving. One reason cited for the uproar was the lack of understanding of RCA polity. The African-American clergy who were recruited to support the missions in the South in the late 1800s and early 1900s worked primarily with people who had no prior knowledge of Reformed polity. However, because the African-American Council labored to educate and train leaders, many of the black congregations of the late twentieth century had very strong and informed leaders heading their churches. The traditions that had an abundance of black ministers had polity and theology which were very different from the RCA. While they may have shown tremendous potential for ministry and were brilliant leaders, many of these ministers had a style of leadership that clashed with what the RCA congregations understood and would accept. As a result, many congregations experienced schisms of varying degrees. Smith cited this as one of the major reasons several black congregations are still struggling today. While the community continues to change around them and the potential for ministry is visible in abundance, the church's financial situation and poor attendance remains a burden because many congregations are still in the process of recovering and healing.[36]

The Reverend Dr. Glen Missick, the current executive director of the African-American Council, has made the task of recruiting black ministers to the RCA one of his primary goals. During his first year, he traveled from church to church, worshiping and meeting with congregations. He has learned about the history of many of our congregations and has had an opportunity to witness the potential that exists for congregations who can attract pastors with a clear vision and an appreciation for Reformed polity. In light of this, Missick says he is working with the regional synods and the Office of Urban Ministry to begin designing orientation workshops for ministers interested in serving in the RCA.

Smith believes the African-American Council needs to focus on youth in order to build a strong foundation. From its beginning, the council has encouraged and included the voices of young people within the structure of their body. Over the years, this has developed into a full youth forum at the annual caucuses, in which young people from all over the denomination can gather to discuss and share issues of relevance to them. It has also provided fertile ground for the training of youth leaders.

In the end, black people have found a home in the RCA. They can raise their children and work to spread the gospel of Jesus Christ in the context in which they live.

36 Smith interview.

5

Northern Exposure: New York Synod in the Mid-Hudson

Scott Conrad and Stephen Hanson

The story of the upper Mid-Hudson Valley and the Particular Synod of New York begins in 1826, when the Classis of Poughkeepsie, given away to Albany Synod by the General Synod of 1812, was returned to the southern synod. In that year, the burning question in Poughkeepsie Classis was the place of the *Heidelberg Catechism* in the life of the church.

> Classis would respectfully inquire of the General Synod, through Particular Synod, whether the Article of the Constitution, requiring the regular exposition of the catechism on a part of every Lord's day, is to be rigidly enforced, or whether it may not be submitted to consistories when circumstances may require it to be partially dispensed with.[1]

New York Synod, in its response, insisted that asking this question appeared to acknowledge a delinquency on the part of churches in the classis concerning this constitutional requirement.

---

1 *Acts and Proceeding of the Particular Synod of New York* (hereafter referred to as *MPSNY*), 1826, 5.

With the arrival of the 1830s, the churches of Poughkeepsie Classis were concerned primarily with seeing revival of some kind in their congregations and communities. The May, 1831, report seemed to capture the prayers that were going up to heaven from them at the time:

> Seldom, we believe, if ever, has more fervent supplications [sic] been found ascending to heaven among us, that God would arise, and for His own name's sake, pour out His Spirit in the midst of us, and revive His work; and seeing that God's children take pleasure in Zion's stones and favor the dust thereof.[2]

Though the churches used the language of the revivalists of their day, there is no evidence that the congregations of the classis used the methods commonly thought of when we consider that century's revivals. When mentioning the awakening at the church in Poughkeepsie, which was "still advancing" in 1831 for the previous year, the State of Religion report of the classis claims, "It has gone on without excitement or confusion. The means employed have been of the ordinary kind."[3] The classis seemed to be allaying any fears that they were straying from accepted Dutch Reformed forms and methods to achieve revival.

Although the 1830s didn't see "extensive revivals of religion" within the bounds of Poughkeepsie Classis, the opening of the decade did find revival in the Poughkeepsie church, with 142 adults professing Christ's name during 1831 and 1832. In 1832, the Church of Linlithgo was visited by the Lord with "a copious shower of blessing,"[4] adding fifty-three to the full communion of that congregation upon confession. In 1838, the classis reported:

2   *MPSNY,* 1831, 23.
3   Ibid.
4   *MPSNY,* 1832, 10.

...(W)e gather the cheerful intelligence, that the Lord has come down to visit the people of Hopewell, together with their offspring, by the outpouring of his spirit, until the rich and poor, the thoughtless and sober, are asking, with affecting anxiety, for the ways of Zion, and the paths of truth.[5]

Other concerns of the day included helping the cause of temperance progress, ensuring that the Monthly Concert of Prayer be faithfully maintained, and that the progress of Sabbath-breaking, especially for pleasure, be arrested. The classis also tried to ensure that foreign missions received "gladdening attention" in its congregations, that preaching from the Heidelberg Catechism not be neglected, and that a uniform system of "Sabbath-school instruction" be devised. In 1831, the Church at Kingston was transferred to the Classis of Ulster—then in the Synod of Albany— and, in 1837, the classis both received the Germantown Reformed Church under its care and organized a new congregation at Glenham. By 1837, the classis reported, "While none of their congregations have been privileged to experience any extraordinary visitations of saving mercy, yet the general condition of the churches is well adapted to strengthen their hands and encourage their hearts."[6]

The early years of the 1840s saw that desired revival come to many of the churches in the Classis of Poughkeepsie.

The nursery of the Church is a judicious system of awakening sinners to a perception of the healing power of the Gospel of salvation...it speaks most decidedly in the still small voice—this unstops the ear, and its communications break the heart and bind it up with the healing balm of the Great Physician. We are glad to learn that such awakenings have occurred.[7]

5   *MPSNY,* 1838, 12.
6   *MPSNY,* 1837, 11.
7   *MPSNY,* 1842, 8-9.

Poughkeepsie was one of three classes that were noted particularly for the awakenings within their boundaries. This classis reported, "God has appeared with power and grace," especially in Fishkill and the newest church of the classis, Glenham.[8] Its numbers increased to seventy and its debt was nearly paid off. By the following year, revivals of greater or lesser degree were reported at Rhinebeck, Germantown, Linlithgow, Greenport, Poughkeepsie, and Hopewell.

In 1844, the propriety of dancing was debated in the classis, and a resolution was forwarded to New York Synod for its consideration.

> *Whereas*, dancing as an amusement, has among its advocates some professed followers of Christ, who pronounce it an innocent and harmless recreation...and
>
> *Whereas*, this amusement is by many of Christ's professing friends much condemned...
>
> *Resolved*, That the whole subject be referred to Particular Synod, to take such action upon it as in their judgment shall seem best.[9]

Dry Spells and Reawakenings

But if the early 1840s brought words of promise and hope, the tone was changing by the middle of the decade. In 1845, the classis sent this strong expression of lament to the synod:

> Pastor after pastor has been heard putting forth the melancholy exclamation, "Who has believed our report," &c. [sic]; and church after church has been heard complaining that citizens of the heavenly Jerusalem have too much forgotten their character as denizens of that holy commonwealth.[10]

The remaining years of the decade echoed much the same sentiments. In 1847, "The Word of God seems to fall like rain on

8   *MPSNY,* 1842, 10.
9   *MPSNY,* 1844, 31.
10 *MPSNY,* 1845, 9.

the rock, and spiritual barrenness prevails...."[11] In 1848, "We have much, also, to deplore, and to make us exclaim—'Our leanness!'"[12] They lamented the prevalence of worldliness and lukewarmness. This woe continued into the next decade. In 1854, this sad song was still being sung; the synod report stated: "Many lamentations come up to us over prevailing sins such as intemperance, Sabbath-breaking, and a general spirit of worldliness, and over the absence of the spirit of the Lord in general awakening and revival."[13] Poughkeepsie's 1857 report concluded, "If Religion does not advance there must be delinquency in regard to the all-important duty of prayer," echoing a statement made by the synod on the subject in 1850: "In review of the whole, it is most manifest, that we need more, far more, of the spirit of prayer...."[14]

Despite the general feeling of lament, and the "saddened hearts" of pastors, there could also be found "a pleasant and hopeful spirit" in the churches of the classis.[15] In 1847, a new church was organized in Poughkeepsie, "under the most favorable auspices."[16] In 1854, the churches at Hopewell and Rhinebeck were encouraged by large accessions. By the end of the decade, all the reports were much brighter in tone. In 1858, it was reported that almost all the congregations in Poughkeepsie Classis were united in experiencing increases of both numbers and graces.

> In all our goodly heritage, peace and harmony have reigned; large and solemn audiences have attended on the services of God's house; the spirit of liberality has increased; prayer meetings have multiplied; the Holy Spirit has been poured out on some of our churches, and none have been without evidence of his gracious presence.[17]

11 *MPSNY,* 1847, 7.
12 *MPSNY,* 1848, 8.
13 *MPSNY,* 1854, 7.
14 *MPSNY,* 1850, 7.
15 *MPSNY,* 1851, 7.
16 *MPSNY,* 1848, 16. This was the Second Reformed Church. Edward Tanjore Corwin, *Manual of the Reformed Church in America,* 4th ed. (New York: Board of Publication of the Reformed Church in America, 1902), 1022.
17 *MPSNY,* 1859, 24.

This period also saw the formation of the Classis of Hudson in 1846, taking four congregations from the Synod of Albany and four from the Synod of New York. There was talk of transferring this new Classis to Albany in 1847, but it ended up remaining within New York's bounds. In 1847, the Church of Taghakanic was transferred from Classis Poughkeepsie to the new Classis of Hudson.

Members of both classes continued to yearn for revival among their members. In 1860, the Second Church of Poughkeepsie reported,

> From time to time we have had evidence of God's Spirit among us, and some precious souls have been led publicly to confess Christ. Within a few weeks we have been encouraged to believe that there is more than ordinary interest among the people of God. They have been revived, and a spirit of more earnest prayer has prevailed.[18]

But many of the reports from this period still sing a song of lament, with words such as, "It is not our privilege to speak of great things as to large ingatherings of souls,"[19] "We have not been permitted to rejoice over a revival of religion,"[20] "Nothing cheery to report,"[21] and "We have reason to mourn spiritual barrenness."[22]

Despite these laments, the reports of this period generally related that attendance at Sunday worship was good, prayer meetings were well maintained, and "Sabbath-schools" were showing much progress. Yet, because people donated more toward local causes in connection with the Civil War, the usual giving to church benevolence and missions was not what it had been prior to the outbreak of the conflict. The first five years of the 1860s can be summed up in the words of First Church of Poughkeepsie's 1861

---

18 *MPSNY,* 1860, 23.
19 *MPSNY,* 1860, 24.
20 Ibid.
21 *MPSNY,* 1861, 24.
22 *MPSNY,* 1863, 13.

report: "Nothing of a special nature has occurred with them during that year."[23]

In 1866 and '67, many of the churches in the Classis of Hudson rejoiced over revival in their midst. The Church of Hudson reported that, through a week of prayer in January, subsequent prayer meetings, and personal conversations with seekers, excitement about the faith increased. The Second Church of Claverack also spoke of a "refreshing from the Lord's presence," beginning in the winter of 1865 and continuing into 1866. Linlithgo, likewise, reported an outpouring of the Lord's Spirit. By 1867, this outpouring seems to have spread. Hudson, Second Claverack, and Linlithgo continued to declare "this work of the Spirit is still going on," and "the influence of the season of refreshing has not ceased to be felt."[24] These congregations were joined by Claverack, Greenport, Germantown, and Greenbush in proclaiming an awakening among their members. These awakenings or revivals resulted in larger attendance at prayer meetings and the creation of new prayer meetings, new converts joining these churches, and an increase in benevolences.

The churches in the city of Poughkeepsie also reported "a time of refreshing from the presence of the Lord"[25] in 1866. They still spoke of the fruits of revival in 1867, as did the Rhinebeck congregation, which reported a spiritual refreshing in the winter of 1866 that was carried over into prayer meetings in 1867.

After two years of revival, things seem to have quieted down again in all the congregations of Poughkeepsie and Hudson classes. Overall, the congregations closed the decade with good feelings. Although the spiritual condition was not at the heightened level of 1866-67, there was general agreement that there was cause for much gratitude to God for "tokens of the Holy Spirit's presence." In particular, "Sabbath-schools" throughout the two classes flourished.

23 *MPSNY,* 1861, 24.
24 *MPSNY,* 1867, 13.
25 *MPSNY,* 1866, 32.

The Millbrook Reformed Church was organized by the Classis of Poughkeepsie in 1867 as a missionary effort of the classis. It was expected that long patience and much prayer would be needed if this church were to grow, and then that it would grow slowly, because the community was perceived to have little concern for matters of faith.

The year 1870 brought the long-desired awakening in some of the churches of the region. Greenport, in Hudson Classis, spoke of the work on the "unregenerate" being first manifest in early February and continuing into the year. The Church of Dashville Falls in the Kingston Classis (which had been organized among the congregations of Bloomingdale, Clove, Dashville Falls, Guilford, Hurley, Second Kingston, Marbletown, New Paltz, North Marbletown, Rochester, Rosendale, and Samsonville in 1856)[26] rejoiced that thirty-four new members were received into its communion, and St. Remy reported "an awakening interest in things pertaining to God."[27] Over in Poughkeepsie Classis, Hyde Park spoke of enjoying a season of refreshing, and Fishkill a revived spirit of prayer. Many of these awakenings or refreshings of the Spirit apparently came out of the week of prayer that was held in the early part of each year during most of the nineteenth century.

Hudson Classis constituted a new congregation in 1871, the Livingston Reformed Church at Linlithgo. Temperence was still a concern among many of the churches. In 1874, New Paltz spoke of a union temperance meeting having been recently established and "earnestly sustained." In 1878, First Church of Claverack reported:

> ...considerable work has been done in the work of temperance in our community. Many have been induced to sign the total abstinence pledge, and we have reason to

---

[26] Edward Tanjore Corwin, *A Digest of Constitutional and Synodical Legislation of the Reformed Church in America* (New York: Board of Publication of the Reformed Church in America, 1906), 363.

[27] *MPSNY,* 1870, 11.

believe not a few have been redeemed from the habit of using intoxicating liquors.[28]

The 1870s also saw the introduction of a new "envelope system" in some of the churches. "Sabbath-schools" continued to flourish and prosper as they had since the congregations embraced them in the early part of the century.

By 1878, new groups started to develop which would have a large impact on mission awareness and benevolent giving in the region. In Second, Kingston, and New Paltz in Kingston Classis, auxiliaries to the Women's Board of Foreign Missions were formed among women of the congregations. The following year, New Hackensack and Hyde Park in Classis Poughkeepsie spoke of increases in mission giving, mainly due to these new women's groups dedicated to missions. The movement continued to grow into the 1880s. Clove Church organized a Women's Missionary Society in 1886. First and Second Claverack, Livingston, Upper Red Hook, and Marbletown spoke of forming such societies in 1888. By the end of the decade, nearly all of the churches in the region had women's groups, all committed to mission work.

In 1886, there was also the first mention of a new youth organization being formed among the churches of the valley. Christian Endeavor took off like wildfire and, as with the women's groups, within ten years almost all the congregations were reporting great things concerning it. Kingston Classis reported in 1890, "Some four or five Christian Endeavor Societies have been founded during the year, and their success shows the efficiency of this agency in training the young disciple to labor 'for Christ and His Church.'"[29] A few parishes also spoke of the "King's Daughters," a discipleship group designed for young women and children.

The final decade of the century seems to have been a blessed one for most of the churches in the region. Most reported steady growth over those years. A few congregations experienced years that were

28 *MPSNY,* 1878, 10.
29 *MPSNY,* 1890, 13.

"specially blessed." In 1891, New Paltz received sixty-nine people on confession, partially as a result of evangelistic services held in various parts of the region. In 1892, Millbrook spoke of a gain of forty-five members. In 1845, Fair Street Church, Kingston, rejoiced over what it called "one of the most prosperous years in its history," reporting an "ingathering" of fifty, and more who were ready to unite at the next Communion.

These years saw the start of some new congregations. Kingston Classis organized the church at Gardiner. In 1892, 123 members of Second Church, Claverack, in Hudson Classis organized a new congregation at Philmont. The congregation of Rosendale Plains was organized by the Classis of Kingston in November of 1897.

Some congregations reached out to nearby communities, creating mission or satellite congregations with the building of chapels. The Livingston Church of Linlithgo conducted, in 1892, what it called "promising and needed work at the chapel at Benden Mines, ministering to its workers." First, Claverack, was building a Memorial Chapel in the center of the village in 1893, for Sabbath school and prayer meeting purposes. In 1898, a mission Sunday school was organized in the southwestern part of the city of Poughkeepsie by Second, Poughkeepsie. The following year, the congregation erected Immanuel Chapel.

By 1898, reports were more mixed. Churches in the Classis of Hudson reported slight decreases in every department except for the Sunday school. Kingston Classis, on the other hand, reported an increase in membership within its bounds. The effects of a widespread economic depression that hit the country in the mid-1890s, while it did not immediately affect giving, had, by this time, hurt benevolent giving throughout the region.

As the decade and the century came to a close, the Classis of Kingston offered up this prayer, which seemed to capture the hopes and desires of the time.

> Our prayer is, that the sun of righteousness may shine on us, that the gracious rain and the covenant-bow may salute us

and all receive new light, life, and fruitfulness. So will the words be true of us too. "And I will dwell in you and walk among you; and I will be your God and ye will be my people. And I will be a Father unto you and ye shall be my sons and daughters, saith Jehovah Almighty."[30]

The optimism of the 1890s was replaced with the pessimism of the 1900s. Words like evangelism and outreach vanished. Churches reported holding their own at best. The dawn of the twentieth century was a time of treading water for the Upper Hudson Valley Synod of New York churches. For some, like High Falls, it was a time of severe economic hardship. That congregation reported deep losses because of the decline of the cement industry and the closing of the Delaware & Hudson Canal. Not until 1908 did evangelistic activity resume in the northern reaches of the synod. Not all membership declines were accurate however; many rolls were purged in response to the mandates of the General Synod, which insisted that churches put their membership rolls in order. And so they did.

From Optimism to the Great War

The Upper Hudson Valley was established territory for the Reformed Church in the sense that there was little in the way of new church starts. The one exception seems to have been the work of the Classis of Poughkeepsie. In 1911, the classis reported that a new church had been established in Arlington,[31] the first church start reported anywhere in many a year. It would not be their last.

The early years of the decade were also marked by a renewed interest in missions; in fact, there was an interest in almost anything to do with missions, either foreign or domestic. In 1911, for instance, the Gardiner church reported increased gifts to foreign missions, and Fair Street, Kingston, proudly proclaimed its work in its own City of Kingston Mission. The New Paltz and Clove

30 *MPSNY,* 1899, 16.
31 *MPSNY,* 1911, 5.

churches were ministering actively to workers building the great
New York City aqueduct, Rosendale Plains established a Women's
Missionary Society, and Rochester announced that "they have
assumed the support of their own missionary, Mrs. Honegger, now
in India." In report after report, the word "mission" appeared. And
this was just the Classis of Kingston.[32] The classis was not unique,
however. That same year, Millbrook established a mission to "the
colored population of the community."[33] The churches went
further, reaching out beyond their traditional white and Dutch base.
Hudson Classis reported the establishment of a Hungarian church
in Hudson with thirty-one members in 1913.[34] Unfortunately, this
experiment was unsuccessful, and the church became a mission of
the established Hudson City church in April, 1918.[35]

Classis lines, which often seem geographically confused, were in
some small part rationalized when Hudson's lone Dutchess County
Church—St. John's in Upper Red Hook—moved to Poughkeepsie
Classis in 1912.[36] The following year, Cold Spring reported "no
services held," and then disappeared from mention. Poughkeepsie
Classis then established its second church start of the decade, again
in Poughkeepsie, founding Emmamuel Church by 1915.[37]

All was not roses in this decade. The synod report on the state of
religion for 1912 reported a decline of 1,087 students in the Sunday
school population from the previous year.[38] The upper Hudson
Valley churches mirrored that concern, but bigger worries were on
the horizon. The decade closed with the United States being drawn
into the "Great War." Mission activity by churches ceased. Many
reported their ministers engaged as chaplains or in other war work.
Other fights were on the table too. The synod came down squarely
in favor of Prohibition and was distressed by the "Sabbath

32 *MPSNY,* 1911, 17-20.
33 *MPSNY,* 1911, 54.
34 *MPSNY,* 1913, 17.
35 *MPSNY,* 1918, 17.
36 *MPSNY,* 1912, 55.
37 *MPSNY,* 1915, 43.
38 *MPSNY,* 1913, 10.

desecration" of movie theaters and baseball games. As the decade closed, First and Second Poughkeepsie churches combined, later building a new edifice on Hooker Ave.[39]

The Roaring Twenties

Once the War was over, a nation turned to peace and prosperity. Optimism ruled. Churches, too, reported peace dividends. In a single year, 1920, the number of members joining by confession increased by 35 percent in the synod.[40] The valley churches prospered as well. For the same year, Hudson Classis reported a jump in benevolent offerings from $5,071 to $9,103.[41] Growth occurred in all other categories, too.

A major realignment of classis and synod churches was on the 1922 agenda,[42] and it was structured rather curiously. For centuries, some churches in Ulster County were members of the Classis of Kingston, Particular Synod of New York, while others were members of the Classis of Ulster, Particular Synod of Albany. In a noble attempt to straighten out classis boundaries, but using a rather clunky procedure—certainly not decently and in order—it was proposed that the Classis of Kingston be transferred in its entirety to the Synod of Albany, merged with their Classis of Ulster under that name, and then transferred back to the Classis of New York as the new Classis of Ulster. New York Synod worried what would happen if its sister synod, now nicely enlarged, refused to transfer this new Ulster Classis back. In spite of efforts to deny the whole process, the new Classis of Ulster was welcomed in 1923.[43] This was not the last transaction between these two particular synods; some Classis of Ulster churches were later transferred to Greene Classis.

---

[39] *MPSNY,* 1919, 41.
[40] *MPSNY,* 1920, 11.
[41] *MPSNY,* 1921, 13.
[42] *MPSNY,* 1922, 62-63.
[43] *MPSNY,* 1923, 10.

But with the war over, the interest in missions was back. In 1921, Poughkeepsie reported the establishment of an Italian Mission in the United States,[44] while 1924 marked the first mention of the latest British import: Rhinebeck noted that a Boy Scout troop had been established at their church during the year.[45] The valley churches also began sprucing themselves up; numerous property improvements were noted in their reports. Some churches tried bold new moves: home visitation and evangelism programs were reported to be great member-builders by those who tried them. Some couldn't. In 1929, the Classis of Poughkeepsie reported that it was being adversely affected by a shortage of clergy.[46] Four churches had vacant pulpits. Soon, however, there were bigger problems to deal with. By the end of the decade, reports were starting to come in of declines in members and in giving, the first signs that the Great Depression was taking hold. Emmanuel Church, founded in 1915, is listed for the last time in this classis report.

The Great Depression through World War II

The churches of the Upper Hudson Valley showed a real spirit of optimism during the first few years of the depression. They faced bravely forward. They continued on as the economic bite deepened. If the reports to synod are to be believed, they even found a silver lining behind the dark cloud. Many reported a spiritual revival. There was no getting around the financial impact of the depression, yet their rhetoric had a real tone of optimism. Some, like New Paltz in its May 1934 report, even injected a little humor. "We have tried to plant some seed. Our first plan this year is to keep our heads above water."[47] Few would have gone as far as Rhinebeck, however, who stated that same year, "This past year a most delightful one

---

44 Edwin Coon, *Old First: a History of the Reformed Church in Poughkeepsie, New York*, 79.
45 *MPSNY*, 1924, 43.
46 *MPSNY*, 1929, 36.
47 *MPSNY*, 1934, 22.

from every standpoint—an excellent spirit of cooperation and activity."[48] They did reflect the common attitude to the financial malaise of the time however, as they continued, "Our finances are a problem yet they are not nearly so difficult as most and no problem at all compared to many." By 1935, the Depression had clearly taken its toll; the brave and optimistic tone had been replaced with discouraging words. Difficult times were upon them.

It seemed that, as quickly as adversity appeared, it vanished. The following year, much was made of the General Synod program, "Greater Things." Congregations from the three Mid-Hudson Valley classes were energized; a new spirit was in the air. Perhaps the longest report on the state of religion was given for that year, most of the report given over to the Greater Things program. Apparently, just as some New Deal programs used psychology to succeed, this one was a success, too. The churches of the three classes escaped the fates of some of their New York city sisters; none closed during the Depression. Many survived the '30s weakened numerically and financially, but survive they did.

By the later 1930s, things had begun to pick up, but all was not well, for the storm clouds of the war in Europe were growing ever darker. Little mention was made of the conflict that would soon engulf North America. The synod's churches, like the country, were focused inward.

The 1940s opened with a time of quiet growth and revitalization, caused by the prosperity that gripped the region in the late thirties. This period of introspection, of repairing the nation's social and economic structure, faded as the U.S. began to cast a nervous eye toward the events of Europe and the Far East. In the beginning, the valley churches reported increased attendance, a good response in regular offerings and special appeals for war relief and the Red Cross, and overall excellent activity. Pulpits and pews were full. They did not remain so, however. In their 1943 report, the Poughkeepsie church reported "almost 100 of its men and women

48 *MPSNY*, 1934, 18.

serving in the nation's service."[49] Similar reports were filed by others. Dismissals of ministers to become chaplains also began to appear. The valley churches hunkered down for the rest of the war, prayed, and tried to do the work of Christ's church, while the war raged on.

After the war ended, peace and prosperity brought new challenges and new opportunities to the Mid-Hudson Valley churches. It also brought a continuation of the effort to rationalize classes boundary lines. The Jay Gould Memorial Church in Roxbury, Delaware County, was transferred to the Particular Synod of Albany in 1948.[50] In 1949, the synod made its first foray into owning a church camp, voting to take over the Reformed Church interest in a property on Denton Lake in Holmes, New York, which is within the bounds of the Classis of Poughkeepsie.[51] Later, Classis Ulster petitioned the General Synod over a very public spat in the *Church Herald*, which cast doubt on the theological integrity of a Professor at New Brunswick Theological Seminary.[52]

In the matter of church extension, little happened. The areas experiencing peacetime growth in the synod were not in the Hudson Valley, and the focus shifted to areas that were growing, such as Long Island and Westchester, as well as areas that were shrinking, like New York City. The decade closed with a request to study the possibility of uniting two small classes, Hudson, of New York Synod, and the Greene Classis of Albany Synod.[53]

Challenge and Change

The year 1951 marked the release of a major report that would significantly change the northern boundaries of New York Synod.[54] Not only were the churches of Hudson Classis departing to the

49 *MPSNY,* 1943, 15.
50 *MPSNY,* 1948, 6.
51 *MPSNY,* 1949, 14, 34.
52 *MPSNY,* 1949, 38-39.
53 *MPSNY,* 1950, 39.
54 *MPSNY,* 1951, 21-22.

Synod of Albany, forming the nucleus of a new Classis of Columbia, but all non-Ulster County churches in the Classis of Ulster would also be transferred to the north. Later, the proposal was modified such that these churches would form the basis for one new Classis, Columbia-Greene.[55]

There were many issues occupying the mind of the synod in the 1950's, a decade of profound change. Growth finally did come to the northern area of the synod, first to Dutchess, and then to Ulster County. New factories, which produced computers, were built, followed by tracts of new homes. Those churches fortunate enough to be in the path of the builders benefited greatly as new families came, and came on Sundays, as well. Times were good.

The May, 1958, meeting marked the dismissal of Hudson Classis to the Synod of Albany.[56] There were now seven classes in the Particular Synod of New York. The following year, the seeds were planted for another merger, as the Reverend Alvin J. Neevel, field secretary, suggested in his address that the synod study merging the classes of Ulster, Poughkeepsie, and Orange into one new classis.[57]

A consolidation within the Classis of Ulster occurred in 1958; Clove church merged into the Marbletown Reformed Church of Stone Ridge.[58] This was not a time of retrenchment, however, for many churches reported constructing new educational facilities, including twelve churches in Ulster and Poughkeepsie Classis alone, a remarkable number for one year![59]

In the same report, mention was made of eleven churches in the Classis of Poughkeepsie entering into building programs. A spirit of growth and outreach was felt all through the valley. Field Secretary Neevel's suggestion finally bore fruit—final agreement was reached on the consolidation of the Classes of Ulster and Poughkeepsie as the new Classis of Mid-Hudson, which was formally completed as

55 *MPSNY,* 1957, 4.
56 *MPSNY,* 1958, 24.
57 *MPSNY,* 1959, 14.
58 *MPSNY,* 1959, 35.
59 *MPSNY,* 1960, 12.

of January 17, 1967.[60] The following year, three churches of this classis that had been sharing resources formally merged into one, as Bloomington, Rosendale, and Tillson became the United Reformed Church.[61]

Throughout the sixties, membership in the Mid-Hudson Classis continued a slow decline, mirroring the rest of the synod. The merger of the churches mentioned above was cited as a model for other classes to consider. Other churches had already been yoked to save money—Beacon and Glenham, for instance.

At the 1970 meeting of New York Synod, Port Ewen Church fired a salvo in a contentious issue that already involved the entire denomination, an overture from their consistory to allow the ordination of women.[62] Their overture concerned the election of women to consistory. A thornier question was close on its heals: should a woman occupy the pulpit? Perhaps the feelings of the synod were made clearer when, in May, 1971, an overture was approved encouraging classes to consider the ordination of elders, deacons, and ministers of the Word "without regard to sex."[63] A seemingly simple remark in the 1974 synod minutes made Reformed Church history, as Joyce Stedge, a graduate of Union Theological Seminary, answered a call from Rochester Reformed Church in Accord, New York With her October 7, 1973, ordination by Rockland-Westchester Classis, and her October 14 installation as pastor and teacher at Rochester, Joyce Stedge became the RCA's first woman minister,[64] in spite of extended debate at the General Synod, where it was argued that her ordination was irregular. However, since no one from the classis challenged the validity of her ordination, it was upheld.[65]

---

60 *MPSNY,* 1967, 33.
61 *MPSNY,* 1968, 13.
62 *MPSNY,* 1970, 16-17.
63 *MPSNY,* 1971, 12.
64 Program for the Service of Installation of the Rev. Joyce Stedge at Rochester Reformed Church, October 4, 1973.
65 *Acts and Proceedings of the General Synod,* 1974, 481.

The Classis of Mid-Hudson overtured the General Synod to establish a unifying relationship with the United Presbyterian Church, an issue which again developed some controversy. A revised but less formal arrangement was substituted and approved.[66] Mid-Hudson Classis seemed to be quite active in stirring the waters of New York Synod during the seventies. It overtured for one elder and one minister delegate to the synod for each 1,000 members of a classis (it was the second largest classis in 1974),[67] and, at the 1976 meeting, it overtured concerning the ever-popular question of assessments, requesting specifically that the regional synod follow General Synod's guidelines. Once again, a referral to committee was made.[68]

During this time, the synod's budget grew rapidly, with much of the increase being used for aid to churches in need, although only one church from Mid-Hudson was receiving aid. Mid-Hudson, which had established a campus ministry at the State University College at New Paltz, did seek financial assistance to support this ministry.

The mid to late seventies saw some significant growth occurring in a few of the congregations of Mid-Hudson Classis, while most struggled to hold their own and a few began declines which would level off in the mid-eighties. The Cottekill church was closed in 1977. Concerns of the churches were focused on membership. In addressing those concerns, the merits of the church growth movement of the day were debated. As a result of these debates, an overture was sent to the General Synod, asking that the church-growth fundraising drive be suspended until its theological implications could be reviewed.

The high inflation of the late 1970s created another concern. The operating costs of local churches rose tremendously in just five years. As 1980 rolled around, some congregations seemed to be

66 *MPSNY,* 1971, 12.
67 *MPSNY,* 1974, 11-12.
68 *MPSNY,* 1976, 36-37.

focusing their sights and resources inward. As a result of that trend, the president of the classis that year recommended "that we do all we can in the life of our various congregations to overcome a survival syndrome, and keep the larger program of the RCA as an integral response to the calling of Christ."[69]

Concerns about small churches and how to address their particular needs began to take a prominent place in the attentions of the classis. The president's report in 1982 read:

> Our Classis, like many others in the RCA, has a predominance of small churches, and it is time to deal realistically with their specific needs. Therefore, I recommend that the Human Support Committee begin a study of the special needs of the small church, seeking ways that we, as a Classis, can help them face the realities of the present time.[70]

As a result of this recommendation, the classis formed a small-church subcommittee to tackle the issues facing the small church.

As the congregations faced issues that arose close to home, the classis, in 1977, began to look beyond the Hudson Valley toward the Carolinas, and to the potential for starting a new church in the Raleigh-Durham area. It was determined that the community of Cary, outside of Raleigh, had some potential. The Classis of Mid-Hudson threw its prayers and resources behind this new project and, two years later, forty-three people meeting regularly for worship were presented for membership as a congregation of the classis. This group was organized as the First Reformed Church of Cary, North Carolina, which has grown into a vibrant and vital congregation of 237 over the past twenty years. The classis also threw its support behind a church start in Chapel Hill, North Carolina, but, unlike Cary, this congregation never found its niche in the community and, after much prayer and discussion, was discontinued in the mid-nineties.

---

69 Minutes of the Classis of Mid-Hudson, March 18, 1980, 3.
70 Minutes of the Classis of the Mid-Hudson, March 16, 1982, 3.

Innovations

In the early 1990s, the IBM corporation moved out of Ulster County and downsized in Dutchess County, resulting in economic reversals for the region that, in turn, brought drastic reductions in membership and giving for many Mid-Hudson congregations. A few churches have rallied from this economic blow, but most are ending the decade with fewer people in the pews than they had when it began. The 1990s also saw the merger of the North Marbletown Reformed Church with the Community Church of High Falls and the closing of the Lyonsville Reformed Church. As congregations in the Hudson Valley struggled to remain open and keep their pulpits filled, they sought innovative procedures, and the Classis of Mid-Hudson responded with a new, but very old solution: filling pulpits of smaller churches with other than professional, ordained clergy. Following the lead of other denominations, the classis experimented with "preaching elders." At a special meeting in March, 1990, elder Bud Passus was examined and granted permission to serve as "lay stated supply" at the Shandaken Reformed Church, Mt. Tremper.[71]

At the fall meeting, discussion continued concerning what to call this new creation. "Teaching elder" was one suggestion that was considered. Stated supply elders were then serving two churches: North Marbletown and Mt. Tremper. At the classis's annual meeting of 1991, the term "preaching elder" was adopted, after consulting with the synod judicial business committee about how to properly constitute this new entity.[72]

This creation continued to be a source of discussion at almost every classis meeting. Even worse, there appeared to be a conflict with the *Book of Church Order (BCO)*.[73] Still, the classis persisted, resulting in a complaint being filed with the Judicial Business

---

[71] Minutes of the Classis of Mid-Hudson, March, 20, 1990, 1.
[72] Minutes of the Classis of Mid-Hudson, March 19, 1991, 4.
[73] Minutes of the Classis of Mid-Hudson, October 20, 1992, 4.

Committee of the Synod of New York. The Judicial Business Committee found the classis in violation of the *BCO*. Mid-Hudson was to provide an ordained minister or student under care for half of the services at each church.[74] At the same meeting, the classis began the process of overturing the General Synod to legitimatize the "preaching elder," sending the overture along in March 1995. The Commission on Theology issued its report entitled, "The Commissioning of Preaching Elders," to the 1996 General Synod. This report was distributed to the classes for study, revision, and consideration at the 1997 General Synod.[75] "Preaching elders" were adopted for inclusion in the *BCO* in 1998.

The northern boundaries of the Regional Synod of New York have seen many changes during the two hundred years of its existence. Many churches who were members of this synod for most of that time have departed to Albany. Others, members of Albany Synod for most of their existence, are now part of New York's fellowship. Many churches are far older than the synod itself. Some of the changes that now seem everyday were born here, struggled over, and became official only after much difficulty. Yet, through it all, the presence of the Reformed Church in America has remained, and remained vibrant. The possibilities for the next two hundred years are excellent.

[74] Minutes of the Classis of Mid-Hudson, March 16, 1993, 5.
[75] *Acts and Proceedings of the General Synod,* 1996, 391-99.

6

Reflections on Change in the Classis of Queens

Herman D. De Jong

On a beautiful winter day in January of 1964, I was ordained as a minister of the Word[1] at the Steinway Reformed Church, which is located in the Astoria section of the borough of Queens in the City of New York, by the Classis of Queens, RCA. So many people came forward for the laying-on-of-hands that, in spite of the solemnity of the moment, I remember thinking, "I hope I'm not going to be stepped on or have my neck injured by the weight of the hands on my head."

Of course, all of the hands were lily white! Except for the nearby First Reformed Church of Astoria, which had made a transition from an all-white congregation to a primarily all-black congregation in the early 1950s, when I arrived in Queens over thirty-five years ago, there were very few non-white members in the twenty congregations of Queens Classis.[2]

In many regards, in those days, the classis was a reflection of the racial/ethnic make-up of Queens, the second most populous of New York City's five boroughs. Although there were pockets of

[1] Of course, we are now called ministers of Word and Sacrament, but that wasn't the official designation twenty-five years ago.
[2] When describing congregations or people as "white," in this essay, I generally refer to people whose roots are European, more often than not northern European.

African-Americans, Hispanics, and others, Queens was primarily white and Christian, having absorbed immigrants primarily from Europe for over three hundred years. The members of the RCA churches could trace their family roots to a host of nations.

In the 1960s and 1970s, the African-American population in the borough grew rapidly. This population change directly and profoundly affected two of the churches of the classis. The Community Church in Cambria Heights and the First Reformed Church of Jamaica soon became primarily African-American congregations. This in contrast to the RCA congregation in Far Rockaway, which, in the 1950s, sold its building and moved to what it assumed would always be a "safe" white neighborhood. It was disbanded in 1973.

About the time these changes were taking place, I had been elected to the exalted position of stated clerk of Queens Classis, a job I held for nearly eighteen years. Since the job required sitting at the head table, I was able to get a clear look at the folks who came to the classis meetings. I recall being thrilled that elder John Ashley from the First Reformed Church, Astoria, was no longer the only African-American at the meetings; he was joined by such fine people as Elmer Hammond from Cambria Heights, Annie Lee Phillips from Jamaica, and many others.

The 1970s and 1980s was a period of enormous change in the composition of the population of Queens. In many sections of the borough, people moved out and new folks arrived, or, perhaps more accurately, new folks moved in and others took flight. In general, a lot of whites left as increasing numbers of African-American and Hispanic people settled into Queens. Also, due largely to changes in the national immigration laws, a wave of new immigrants arrived from distant shores. Few of those folks were from Europe. Instead, they came from Central and South America: Nicaragua, Colombia, Peru; from the Mid-east: Jordan, Egypt, Lebanon; from Asia: India, Taiwan, Korea. Many of these new arrivals were Christian; many were not.

Of all these, it was the Taiwanese and the Korean immigrants who made the greatest impact on the RCA churches of Queens. Why? Many of them were Protestant Christians whose denominations had historic ties with RCA mission work in Asia. How did the Classis of Queens, an English-speaking, primarily white body, greet these newcomers, brothers and sisters in Christ from Asia?

Welcoming

Generally speaking, this is what happened in Queens Classis in the past twenty years: First, two white congregations were transformed gradually into Taiwanese churches. They were the Winfield Reformed Church in Woodside and the Newtown Reformed Church in Elmhurst. This followed the earlier pattern of the Cambria Heights church and the Jamaica church.

Second, new congregations were established to minister to the waves of new Christian immigrants, especially those from Taiwan and Korea. In almost all instances, the pastor and a core group of followers approached the classis and asked that the pastor become a minister of the classis and the congregation a member of the Reformed Church in America. These were congregations looking for a home. When I was stated clerk of the classis, it was not unusual to have delegations from just such congregations arrive at my door once or twice a month. Many—probably most—were accepted, a few were turned down, and others lost patience with RCA processes and dropped out.

Third, three buildings formerly occupied by white, English-speaking congregations that had been disbanded were turned over to new congregations. The Long Island City Church was given to the Korean Philippo Church. The Ridgewood Reformed Church became the Chiuyang Korean Church. The Second Reformed Church of Astoria building was passed on to the Taiwan Union Christian Church. That last was a moment of both sadness and joy for me. Since I was the stated supply pastor of the Second Reformed Church, I was sad to see that faithful little congregation disbanded, but I was thrilled to see the building occupied by a strong and vibrant new congregation, who just happened to speak Taiwanese! I treasure the graciousness of the Taiwan Union congregation to this day.

Fourth, a number of RCA churches in Queens began to share their buildings with new congregations. The Bowne Street Church in Flushing began to host a Taiwanese congregation. After several years, the two congregations merged. The new congregation has two pastors, one white and one Taiwanese.

Fifth, but certainly not of least importance, many, if not most, churches in Queens Classis have welcomed newcomers into their fellowship, people who simply happened to move into their neighborhood from another part of the city or state, or who immigrated from a distant land. One would be hard put to find a typical 1950s congregation among the churches of Queens in 2000.

If I were being ordained today, there might well be more hands placed on my head, for there are nearly fifty percent more congregations in Queens now than there were in 1964, and the hands certainly would not all be white!

Bumps in the Road

As the twentieth century draws to a close, there is probably no other classis in the denomination that is as diverse as Queens. Thirteen of the churches are primarily white, English-speaking congregations, six are Korean, five are Taiwanese, three African-American, and one is Hispanic. In the fall of 1999, an Indonesian congregation was taken under the care of the classis. I know of very few people who do not rejoice in this diversity.

Although no one else in the classis was aware of it at the time, the request of the Korean Philippo Church in 1979 to become a member of the Reformed Church, and the decision of the classis to welcome it, was very significant. As clerk of classis, I was very involved in this matter (and felt honored to be asked to preach the sermon at the organization service). The classis was well satisfied with pastor John Lee's qualifications and credentials to transfer into the RCA, and the congregation's desire to become an Reformed church was not questioned. There was, however, much concern about the name. The church was determined to keep "Presbyterian" in its name, arguing that it was necessary to attract members. Some members of the classis believed that was inappropriate and could be very confusing. In the end, it was agreed that the church could come into the classis and retain its full name, although on letterhead and other formal locations it was to identify itself as an RCA congregation. In my opinion, this decision was vitally important— pivotal—for it told everyone that we wanted fellow Christians to be a part of us and that, within reason, we would compromise and work out differences together. We wanted to be a welcoming and diverse classis, and where you came from or what language you spoke was not very important.

It probably should be pointed out that these changes over the past twenty-five years or so have not always been easy. Although all congregations share a common faith in Jesus Christ as Lord, there are significant differences of language, traditions, culture, expectations, and others. Although language has often been the first hurdle to block full integration into the life of the classis, traditions, culture, and the like have also been issues with which to deal. I can recall, for example, the agony of interviewing prospective pastors who spoke no English, or explaining that a word of encouragement from someone in authority did not constitute acceptance into the classis, a great disappointment when negotiations did not work out. In spite of obstacles that were sometimes complex, the Classis of Queens has, to its credit, generally welcomed newcomers, and misunderstandings have been resolved.

An ongoing concern for many of us in Queens is leadership in the classis by immigrant members. Some of the pastors and elders seem uncomfortable with English and, not surprisingly, decline leadership roles. This is not to say there have been none; Jon-Duk-Kim and Norman Chang have served as presidents. Perhaps it will take a generation for this goal to be more fully realized. I believe the classis has been, and is, genuinely committed to encouraging greater participation in the classis and synod and denomination by all its member congregations.

Queens is, and has been for many years, the home to a huge number of Hispanic people from many different countries in Central America, South America, and the Caribbean. Indeed, Hispanics are, collectively, the largest ethnic group in the borough by far. One of the greatest disappointments I have long felt is that Queens Classis has been unwilling or unable to carry on significant ministries among our Hispanic sisters and brothers in the faith. In the 1970s, David Boyce and the folks at the Newtown Reformed Church began a low-key ministry to Hispanics who were rapidly moving into their neighborhood, but, in the end, it did not work out. In 1998, pastor Antonio Lopez and the Iglesia de Christo-La Roca were welcomed into the classis...at last. Praise the Lord!

Queens Classis has not been able to provide ministry to all the newcomers in the borough; after all, people who settle in Queens come from over a hundred countries and speak dozens of languages. It is my hope and prayer that, as people settle in our communities, regardless of where they come from, they will be welcomed in all our churches. If, by God's mercy, it seems necessary to establish new churches, I pray that the classis will be given the grace to do so.

Several of the immigrant/ethnic congregations have English-language worship and so on, as well as Taiwanese, Korean, or whatever original language they might speak. One wonders what will happen to these churches after a generation or two, after immigration has declined. Perhaps, once again, there will be a unity of language as well as faith.

I have made no effort in this essay to describe individual congregations, their size, or how each carries out its ministry. The focus has been on demographic changes and the response of the classis to them. As a long-time member of Queens Classis, I rejoice in the ethnic and racial diversity, but regret other changes I have witnessed. I hope that, whatever has happened or will take place in the future, the ministry of the Reformed Church in America in Queens will not fail but flourish, and that God's name will be praised. As my ministry draws to a close, I know this: if I were to be ordained in the year of our Lord 2000, I would hope God would call me to ministry in Queens, New York.

To God Almighty, the Father, the Son, and the Holy Spirit, be all the praise and the glory!

7

Urban Ministries:
A Practical Perspective
Micheal Edwards

The heartbeat of the Reformed Church in America and the Synod of New York is the diversity that can only be sparked in an urban context. Since my childhood, there has always been a feeling in my heart that the Reformed Church is a special place for worship, fellowship, and partnership. It was different from other churches with which my family was associated. My awareness of this grew as I began to participate in Christ's church in missions, in the classis, in the particular (later called regional) synod, and in the General Synod.

This practical view, as it was reflected through my own journey, explored the inner workings of this unique and diverse synod: different, complex, and yet challenging. Is it an impossible view? No, rather it is a view that flows from the colorful rainbow in the midst of our synod and denomination.

I believe that we do little to celebrate what we have as a church. I recalled that, as a member of the General Synod Council, I would hear people saying that we needed to visit other denominations and investigate how they were performing urban ministry. Then, from another corner, I would hear that we needed to get involved in the city and build new ministries there. In my heart I would ask myself, "Are they blind? Can we really support the efforts being made in the

115

Regional Synod of New York? We are doing urban ministry. We don't need to pay large sums to a 'think tank' to study what we are already doing!'"

The Watts Prayer

During the early 1960s, the Classis of New York—with financial help from the RCA Board of North American Missions—employed elder Clyde Watts to work with city congregations as a part-time lay minister. The first objective was to assist white ministers with minority congregations or communities to become sensitive to the needs of other racial groups. The second was to preach in those churches to show our presence in a transitional community. The third was to engage in conversation with the total church concerning the need to bridge racial differences at a time when the Civil Rights Movement was not only a call for justice in American government, but also in the American church.

I recall that, when Watts was asked to undertake this responsibility, he prayed and prayed. He felt, after serving in organized labor for years in the tobacco fields, that the Lord God was, all along, preparing him for this ministry. He believed also that God wanted him to become involved in the organization of evangelical events. He meditated day and night. He spoke to several ministers, black and white. After praying with the Reverend Don DeYoung, he felt that God had truly called him to a lay pastoral role.

What a day for rejoicing! He was biblically knowledgeable, and he learned the RCA structure quickly. After several weeks of education and preparation, he was on the battlefield for his Lord. He would visit churches and train consistory members regarding the importance of knowing the Bible and the *Book of Church Order*. He would speak to youth groups throughout the city and encourage them to further their education beyond high school. He challenged them to think about a vocation in Christian ministry. He recommended many young people to RCA colleges and seminaries. His part-time employment became a full-time joy. He would visit homes (never afraid to travel alone in the less exclusive areas of the city) and encourage families to join in fellowship with the nearest Reformed Church congregation. He invited strangers and those who sought hope into Christian fellowship. He held street-corner evangelical services and, as his ministry grew, other joined him in these efforts.

Without any formal education from any accredited theological institution, Watts learned to do Christian ministry. Many of our African-American and Hispanic members joined various RCA churches because of his love and witness for Jesus Christ.

The excitement was not just an African-American experience, but a ministry of new concepts for the whole community. Blacks and Hispanics became the focus of a new type of ministry in the various corners of New York City. Elder Maria Garcia, from Elmendorf Reformed Church, assisted with the Spanish interpretation and conducted Spanish services. The prayers of Clyde Watts have enabled the Word of God to be shared throughout the world, and especially in the world of New York City.

A man without any formal education began to touch many souls. Pastors would call on him constantly to preach during their vacations, or whenever the Spirit allowed him. Without a car, he traveled from church community to church community. He wasted no time. He believed that God had a special plan for him when people said, "Free at last! Free at last! Thank God Almighty, we're free at last!"

Watts's prayer was that the Reformed Church would open its eyes to the opportunities of greater missions and ministries, in the city and at home. Before his death, he was able to witness the growth of many inner-city ministries. He was proud to see the sincerity of church leaders who were willing to take risks in the city for the Lord's sake.

The Emergence of the City

By the end of the 1960s, African-American and Hispanic ministers started to appear in the Reformed Church. Classes became sympathetic to the requirements of minorities. There were classes that made it less difficult for minorities to become ministers in the RCA. Some classes accepted these ministers' ordination certificates without investigating whether or not these certifications were from recognized ecumenical institutions. Some of these ministers were installed with the understanding that they would further their education in the joint Master of Divinity program run by New Brunswick Theological Seminary and New York Theological Seminary.[1] Others attempted to fill the requirements by participating in correspondence or unaccredited degree programs.

The sad part was that many ministers and elders knew that the completion announcements for these theological programs were less well regarded by those who legitimately fulfilled their educational objectives. Often, these announcements of completion were accepted to lessen the tension involved in recruiting and securing qualified minorities. Classes did not want to confuse matters between congregations and consistories and those ministers who opted not to fulfill their requirements. As ministers became available, many strove to meet the RCA standard, while others used the situation as an opportunity for social-class mobility in the church community.

Many churches grew with caring and sincere ministers. DeWitt and Elmendorf maintained English and Hispanic ministries, meeting those new challenges in changing communities in the 1970s and early 1980s. New Lots, Elmendorf, Mott Haven, DeWitt, and Grace Reformed churches tapped into educational programs, such as day care, to meet the needs of single and married parents in their communities. Mott Haven formulated the concept of a mini Crystal Cathedral of sorts to beautify the South Bronx. The congregation also joined with the city of New York to assist financially in the formation of a new multi-service center and housing for Headstart

---

[1]   The joint program between New Brunswick and New York seminaries ran from 1975 to 1982. It was a predecessor to New Brunswick's current program at St. John's University in Queens. See Howard G. Hageman, *Two Centuries Plus* (Grand Rapids, Mich., Eerdman's, 1984), 194 ff.

programs for the community. As funds became available from the public and private sectors, the church began to tap into those funded programs, not fully understanding many of the consequences that would follow.

Ministers and Managers

As ministers attempted to meet the educational and social service needs of their members, they found themselves in new roles. Instead of being pastors, they became program directors. They consistently met several times every week with funding sponsors to make certain that all the programs were in compliance with all the regulations. They also had to prepare budgets. Many of the grants defined their scope as non-sectarian; pastors then had to promote programs in the community through non-members rather than bear witness to the love of Christ Jesus. They promoted programs and became advocates of social causes at community planning board meetings and community-based agencies. Many of them had to learn to become politicians in order to secure the endorsement of government officials. Towards the end of each fiscal year, the pastors had to write new grant applications.

Pastors felt more pressure to respond to social issues than to many of the spiritual and religious issues of the church. Some theological principles became minimized and, in some cases, compromised. Consistories were pleased with the revenue coming into their churches. Members were also able to attend conferences and secure employment opportunities within the church.

As funds started to diminish in the mid-1980s, pastors were overwhelmed, and many succumbed to burn-out. Some transferred to other churches. Some changed ministerial approaches. Some took early retirements from their ministries. Some went into specialized ministries. Some suffered from strokes and other medical problems, while some faced not only declining churches, but tensions within their own families. Spouses left for new communities or returned to their parents' homes. Divorce and remarriage became the new norm for family values.

Sadly, the churches suffered. Pastoral leadership was limited to making a name in the community, or to promoting programs that had died for lack of funding. Consistories were not educated in the pastoral and spiritual care of the congregation. In some cases, even as many elders and deacons told their pastors to "take it easy," they were unwilling to assist the pastors in roles that might sustain many of their churches. Consistories became more dependent upon human leadership—pastors—than upon spiritual partnership in ministries. When pastors dissolved their relationships with their congregations, members complained about the messes they had been left. There was no money, no clear power structure, no sense of direction, no ownership, and no knowledge of the past, present, or future of the church. Classes had to close many churches because of the tremendous financial crises in those communities. They also had to face political, social, and economic transitional trends.

Thank God for the New York Synod staff and the racial-ethnic council executives who struggled with most of our congregations in transition. New York Synod raised funds to prevent churches from closing. The councils provided leadership training to consistories and congregations.

From Misunderstanding to Understanding

As the Synod of New York began to reach out into the city, and as the racial-ethnic councils were addressing the problems within those churches, conflicts began to arise. Churches needed leadership development and assistance in understanding their roles in the larger church. At the same time, they needed financial assistance to maintain the tremendous daily expenses of the old "cathedrals" (traditional church structures) they had inherited. At one point, these churches had been self supporting. When the working, middle-class membership moved to the suburbs, however, the expenses to sustain ministry in the city became overwhelming.

Primarily, city churches wrestled with two supportive bodies: the councils, who encouraged churches to examine self-supporting models, and the synod, which found funds to support minority pastors. Consistories and congregations acknowledged that they had made mistakes in the past, but they insisted that they wanted to control their own direction. Pastors became aligned to the synod, and some denounced the councils' training efforts. The congregations and consistories were eager to learn Reformed polity. Pastors and consistories differed, in some respect, and the synod executive and the racial-ethnic executives pursued two different approaches to strengthening churches. Pastors were pleased to have their salaries supported by synodical grants, but consistories did not want to be placed in secondary roles in the region or the denomination. Some pastors began to look down on their colleagues, as if to say, "You go ahead and struggle with being self-reliant. I have mine." In my opinion, those who struggled became the pastors who cared very much about their congregations. Those pastors who relied on the synod to do for them became dependent upon the great white father figure to guide them in deciding what to do in their own communities. Both groups of leaders wanted to strengthen churches in the city, but they never understood how to overcome their own differences.

At the same time, there were distinctions between those white congregations that were able to be self-supporting and those who opted to work in a "strange land." White ministers left many of our churches and went to more prosperous fields, while others remained to serve the urban community. Many of those who remained made an enormous impact on the people of the city, while those who departed lost their master-king image as "The Great White Hope."

As African-Americans observed this class system, they realized that they were being treated as mission churches, rather than as equals in God's kingdom. There were strong voices, especially from the racial-ethnic councils, advocating self-reliance. African-American and Hispanic congregations felt the need to become self-supporting. These churches learned the *Book of Church Order* overnight and insisted upon their right to be included in the policy-making and mission of the RCA. Urban congregations stated clearly that they did not want to be treated as missions, but that they wanted to be able to serve God and people without being labeled.

In the mid-1980s, inner-city churches brought a new look of diversity to New York Synod. No longer were there token representations, but members of many cultures representing their own classes. Councils invited regional and denominational leaders to fellowship with them at their annual caucus conferences. But, by this time, new leadership had formed in churches and synods and councils, and many pastors returned to their original church homes. Some of our churches were in worse condition than before. The resulting political identification hurt the church in some aspects but did not destroy it.

The Elmendorf Opportunity Center

A new chapter in my family relationship with the Elmendorf Reformed Church opened with the birth of the Opportunity Center. When the New York City Teachers' Union had its first strike and the schools were closed in the early 1960s, concerned teachers from the district asked the Elmendorf church to open its doors to them on a full-time basis to educate children. Volunteers from various congregations, interfaith groups, and educators came together to provide educational enrichment for "us," children in the community.

This educational fever spread to the formation of a continuing education program, called the after-school program, a place to help us with homework and remediation. I recall several staff members and volunteers who were involved, such as Janette Johnson and Pauline Atwood, RCA staff members who were also available to assist the Elmendorf Church staff (under the Board of North American Missions), and our own church members. This staff worked diligently with the school system and the community, along with elders Clyde Watts, Ira Blacke, and Maria Garcia, promoting educational enrichment within the East Harlem community throughout the sixties and early seventies.

In the mid-1960s, the program expanded its educational services to form a summer day camp. The summer experience, in conjunction with the Neighborhood Youth Corps, ManPower, Interfaith, the Bronxville Reformed Church, and mission support from the RCA, helped to shape a productive summer experience. The summer included Vacation Bible School, reading and mathematics enhancement, and trips to state parks. Many of us may remember the free buses, which came every Thursday for six weeks.

My favorite experience involved two young tutors named Belinda and Dorothy. They would arrive daily and lead us in Christian songs like, "Them Bones." Others, such as Elder Watts, would encourage us with the love of God. Pastor Donald DeYoung would instruct us with Bible stories. Mrs. Perry would cook our meals. Tom and Bill—who later became pastors in the Synod of New York—served as social workers. Sometimes, Mrs. Clark would bake her famous coconut cake. My mother would help out whenever she could. Mrs. Townsend would remind us about proper behavior. Mrs. O. Flimsier and Mrs. P. Jones became adult supervisors and assistant directors in the program. They were stern individuals, yet very caring, and they worked hard to shape positive character in many of us. Later, as the program developed, elder Dorothea Sadler became the art supervisor (I remember many arts and crafts activities from that particular summer), then the assistant director, and finally, in the mid-1970s, the director.

In the late 1960s, the church developed summer camps linked to the Biblical Seminary (known today as New York Theological Seminary), Christian Herald, and the Stony Brook Schools. Christian Herald offered many opportunities for students to attend Mott Lawn Christian Camp and the Stony Brook "Sunshine Acre." These camps also provided biblical instruction every June for about a decade.

Since then, the program has expanded beyond the church walls. It now contracts space from Community School District Four, using buildings such as Public Schools Seven and Ninety-six during the summer. The program works closely with the district and with Upward Fund Programs to provide swimming and tennis lessons for the children. In 1996, the church opened its first computer lab, dedicated to the memory of the late Pauline Atwood.

As I have grown, so has this program, expanding its educational efforts throughout the community and the city. God has truly blessed this house, the Elmendorf Opportunity Center, and I thank God that my mother had faith in the work of the church educational program all those years ago!

A Sampling of Urban Ministries

Project Hospitality

This ministry was born from the Brighton Heights Reformed Church, which responded to the needs of hungry people on Staten Island by opening a soup kitchen. That ministry provided food to thousands of people. Because of the enormous cry for help in the community, Brighton Heights joined with other concerned churches and the interfaith community to provide an inclusive ministry to the poor. The project now feeds the hungry, shelters the homeless, and provides care and compassion for AIDS patients along with other human services.

Grace Christian Church

This congregation provides a triple ministry, with Chinese, Taiwanese, and English-speaking worship services. This is a unique Asian-American ministry in the heart of Staten Island.

DeWitt Reformed Church

This congregation in lower Manhattan provides a ministry to immigrants. It also reaches out directly to the community with daily activities for seniors, a Headstart Program for over a hundred children a year, a youth fellowship, and pastoral counseling and care opportunities. The members are now thinking about expanding their building or erecting a new facility in the area. On all-you-can-eat buffet days, they provide tasty food at a nominal fee to whoever comes by.

Bethany Memorial Reformed Church

The church provides a ministry to cancer patients and their families, who travel from all over the world to seek help at the Sloan-Kettering Hospital across the street.

The Caribbean Churches

I have had the opportunity to visit our congregations in St. Croix and St. Thomas, and I was impressed with the services they provide: education, food centers, youth programs, and Christian nurture. My wife and I enjoyed our visit to a food mission, called "My Brother's Kitchen." It was an opportunity to help fellow Christians bear witness to God's love.

First Reformed Church, Jamaica

The church as school, or "The Sabbath Concept." It is a reward to observe this church not only showing an interest in education, but also developing new models for educating members through alternative methods of learning God's Word. Christian Education is a strong dimension of the spiritual growth of this congregation.

New Ministries

At one time, there was a rapid increase in the number of Asian-American congregations. Now we are experiencing the emergence of a new group: the Ghanaian churches. These congregations are growing in membership and have already expressed appreciation for the welcome they have received from members of the Reformed Church in America.

The Collegiate Congregations

There is no way to describe the multiple services and programs offered by the Collegiate Church for all our churches and communities. I appreciate their varied styles of worship, from traditional to dramatic, from a classic to a contemporary approach to the Word of God.

Instead of looking to the outside and talking about what and when and how we develop urban ministries in New York City, we need to celebrate the many contributions that our city churches have offered and continue to offer our regional synod and the whole denomination. We need to celebrate the lawyers, doctors, clergy, corporate executives, producers, and other notable leaders in our world who were raised in these congregations from birth to adulthood. We need to celebrate the diversified approach to the Word of God in our worship and praise. We need to celebrate the inclusiveness of our churches. We need to celebrate our congregations when they struggle against the odds through urban trauma, but still bear witness to the love of Jesus. We need to thank God for blessing these churches in the city. Let us all celebrate the victory of our calling!

8

The Asian Church in
the Synod of New York
John E. Hiemstra

One of the most dramatic developments in the Synod of New York over the past twenty years is the expansion of its Asian churches. In 1978, there were just two churches of Asian background in the Reformed Church's Synod of New York. One was the Japanese American United Church; the other was the Winfield Reformed Church in Woodside, Queens.

At that time, the Reverend Albertus Bossenbroek, then executive secretary of the Synod of New York, reported that there was also a Korean congregation in Long Island City and six other Asian tenant congregations meeting in RCA facilities in Queens.[1] None were organized Reformed churches, but their presence was a strong hint of things to come. By 1996, just seventeen years later, twenty-four others were started, bringing the total to twenty-six.

Of these congregations, three were disbanded, leaving a total today of twenty-three, twenty of which are officially organized churches. This does not count an additional half-dozen or so that are in various stages of exploration in the seven classes of the synod, some of which likely will become other new churches. The ministry with Asians has even stretched the Synod of New York geography,

---

[1] *Acts and Proceedings of the Particular Synod of New York* (hereafter referred to as *MPSNY*), 1979, 73.

for one of its new churches is the Boston Taiwanese Church in Framingham, Massachusetts! For more than three hundred years, the RCA was not able to start and sustain a church in New England, until now.

This remarkable growth took place at the same time that membership in Caucasian Reformed churches was in decline. Sometimes the new congregations grew up in the buildings of churches that had closed or were about to close. The growth of the Asian church has is shown in the following Synod of New York statistics, which record increases from 1978 to 1998 in its Asian churches:[2]

Families	1081
Active confirmed members	1473
Total membership	2276
Sunday school enrollment	1071

In previous decades, we sent missionaries to the world. Now those who heard the message are coming to the United States and sharing what they have learned with us. The learners have become the teachers. This certainly seems to be the case in our denomination.

The people to whom the Reformed Church sent missionaries in the nineteenth century are now establishing strong churches among us in the twentieth century. David Abeel went to China in 1842. He was followed by a long list of pastors, medical people, and educators. In 1859, we sent our first five missionaries to Japan. They were followed by many others.[3] In 1984, a New Brunswick Theological Seminary graduate, the Reverend Horace G. Underwood, was sent to Korea as the first ordained Protestant missionary. He had been drawn to commit himself as a missionary to Korea while at New Brunswick Seminary, when he heard an address by the Reverend A. Oltmans, from the Reformed Mission in Japan.[4] This was only two

2   Taken from the *Acts and Proceedings of the General Synod of the Reformed Church in America* (hereafter referred to as *MGS*), 1978 and 1998.
3   Arie R. Brouwer, *Reformed Church Roots* (New York: Reformed Church Press, 1977), 97.
4   Harry A. Rhodes, ed., *History of the Korea Mission*, vol. 1 (Seoul: Presbyterian Church in Korea), 18.

years after the approval of a treaty between Korea, the "Hermit" Nation, and the United States, but pastors who come from Korea often remember his Reformed Church connection, even though he became a Presbyterian. He was followed by dozens of other devoted missionaries, who shared the gospel most effectively. Numerous missionaries were sent to Taiwan after China closed its doors to foreigners in 1950. Immigrants from these nations have now come to America. The descendants of the converts who received the message are now among us declaring and sharing the love of Christ in most powerful ways.

Although we are still referred to occasionally as the Dutch Reformed Church, our ethnic heritage is less evident than it was even a few years ago. Even though the word "Dutch" was dropped from the Reformed Church name more than a century ago, only in recent years has it become noticeable in the faces of our members that we are no longer of white, northern European heritage.

The Asian churches have done much more than increase the number of congregations in the synod. They have brought us a renewed sense of commitment for the sharing of the gospel. The pastors and people of these congregations communicate a strong sense of dedication and sacrifice in the growing of their congregations.

A Listing of the Asian Congregations in the Regional Synod of New York

What follows are the names, dates, and classes of Asian Reformed churches that were established either separately or as entities in previously organized Reformed churches. Those that were subsequently closed are indicated with asterisks. All are in New York unless otherwise noted. Dates refer to the organization of the congregations as churches by their classes:[5]

Manhattan, Japanese American United (New York)	1949
Winfield Taiwanese Reformed Church (Queens)	1969

5   *MGS*, various years.

Long Island City Korean Philippo (Queens)   1979
Elmhurst Newtown Taiwanese (Queens)   1980
Bronx, United W., Korean (Rockland-Westchester)   1981
Manhattan, Chinese Community (New York)   1984
Hastings, Chinese Community (Rockland-Westchester)1984**
Long Island City, Taiwan Union (Queens)   1984
Sunnyside, Nakwon Korean (Queens)   1985
Immanuel/Emmaus Korean (Queens)   1986**
Long Island City, Siloam Korean (Queens)   1985
Williston Park, Formosan (Nassau Suffolk)   1985
Flushing, Bowne Street Taiwanese (Queens)   1987
Ridgewood, Chuiyang Korean (Queens)   1986
Framingham, Mass., Boston Taiwanese (Queens)   1988
Bayside, Shin Kwang Korean (Queens)   1988
Staten Island, Grace Christian Taiwanese (New York) 1990
Flushing, Chuk Bok Korean (Queens)   1992**
Bayside, Taiwanese American (Queens)   1992
Long Island City, Korean (Queens)   1992
Yonkers, Chour Thai (Rockland-Westchester)   1994
Roslyn Heights, New Church, Korean (Nassau-Suffolk)1996
Flushing, Choongsyn, Korean (Queens)   1996
+Scarsdale, Taiwanese (Rockland-Westchester)
      (was Trinity Taiwanese in Ridgewood, Queens)
+Hicksville, Newtown L.I., Taiwanese (Nassau-Suffolk)
+Syosset, Asian American, Multi-Ethnic (Nassau-Suffolk)
+White Plains, United Japanese (Rockland-Westchester)
      **Disbanded
      +Not yet formally organized

A summary shows the following Synod of New York Asian
congregation backgrounds:

Chinese	2
Japanese	2
Korean	11

Taiwanese	9
Thai	1
Asian (multicultural)	<u>1</u>
Total	26

Asian Churches Before 1979

The Japanese American United Church

The oldest Asian church in the Synod of New York is the Japanese American United Church (JAUC), located on Manhattan's Seventh Avenue near Twenty-fourth Street. It is a union church formed as the result of a merger between Reformed and United Methodist bodies in 1953.[6] The two denominations each had mission outreach to Japanese seamen in New York stretching back to the 1890s. The Reformed Church, through the Women's Board of Domestic Missions, established the Japanese Christian Institute in 1894, led by the Reverend Yoshisuke Hirose, and the Japanese Christian Association in 1909, led by the Reverend Atsushi Ohori. These two entities joined to form the Reformed Japanese United Church of Christ in 1949, with the Reverend Giichi Kawamata as the minister.

Just four years later, the Japanese Methodist Church, originally formed in 1901, joined with the new church, because of their long ecumenical cooperation. Together they became the Japanese American United Church in 1953. It is a unique church, formed to serve the small Japanese community in the New York City area. Today, it continues to serve the Japanese people of New York as well as Japanese nationals, many of whom were sent by their Japanese corporations on five-year assignment.

The church reached out to the families of these workers, who were often planted in suburban communities with few friends and little contact with other Japanese families. In each of several outlying towns, home meetings operate as an extension of this

6   *100th Anniversary, The Japanese American United Church, 1893-1993* (New York: Japanese American United Church, 1994), 21.

enterprising church. The number of Japanese in the area is small, and the church serves as an agency to bring them together. The home meetings feature Bible study and assistance to Japanese wives and families as they make adjustments to living in a strange and sometimes confusing country.

The home meetings have been augmented by an ecumenical organization called Special Ministry to Japanese. It also holds home meetings and is designed to minister to Japanese families, as well as to introduce the gospel to them and attempt to bring them to the church, either JAUC or, if their English is sufficient, to other nearby United Methodist, Presbyterian, or Reformed churches. JAUC remains at the center of ministry to Japanese in the New York area. The only other Japanese churches in New York are one Episcopal church in New York and one new nondenominational Japanese church in New Jersey.

The Winfield Reformed Church

The Winfield Reformed Church was established in 1872 as a mission of the Newtown Church in Elmhurst, Queens. It served its community well, but, by the 1960s, many of the families of the church had moved to communities farther out on Long Island. The membership was in decline and the consistory depended upon stated supply ministers for pulpit leadership. In 1969, they invited an energetic bilingual minister, the Reverend Andrew Kuo, of the American Bible Society, to lead their services in English. Because of his Taiwanese background, however, Taiwanese-speaking people were attracted to his ministry. So successful was this ministry to two cultures that when Kuo left Winfield in 1973, a successor was sought who could continue in both languages. The Reverend W.T. Whang served until 1978, after which the Reverend H.C. Bill Lee came to serve the church.

Japanese Church Development

A new United Japanese Church modeled on the JAUC in Manhattan is currently being established in Westchester County. It is an ecumenical partnership between United Methodist, Presbyterian, and Reformed churches that meets in the Hitchcock Presbyterian Church. Like the JAUC, this church also has home meetings and a strong outreach to the Japanese in Westchester County and Connecticut, especially with families who accompany executives assigned to work in the United States for a short period of years. The congregation members are few but highly motivated. With the small immigration of Japanese to the New York area, new church starts among them will be limited. The Reverend Yuri Ando, a United Methodist pastor, was the original missionary pastor invited by the partnership to serve this new church start.

Ministry Among Taiwanese

It was the energetic visionary, the Reverend Bill H.C. Lee, who saw the potential of the Reformed Church to serve Taiwanese people beyond the Winfield Church and proceeded to do something about it. The facilities at Winfield, where he was serving in 1979, were overwhelmed and had no room to expand. He and the minister of the Newtown Church in Elmhurst, the Reverend David Boyce, (another visionary) requested a grant from the Synod of New York to establish a Taiwanese congregation at the Newtown Church. The core of its membership was expected to come from the overcrowded Winfield congregation. Since Lee was aware that the Winfield Church was originally a daughter church of the Newtown Church, he has been heard to say that the new congregation was actually a "granddaughter" church of Newtown.

The Newtown Church became the center of activity for development of Taiwanese churches in the RCA. At one point this mission-minded church had five language congregations worshiping in the church: English, Taiwanese, Korean, Indian, and Indonesian. In addition, the Newtown Church became the mother church of three additional Taiwanese churches: The Taiwanese American Church in Bayside, Queens, the Long Island Newtown Taiwanese Church in Hicksville, Long Island, and the Fairlawn Taiwanese Church in New Jersey.

The outreach of Newtown also included efforts to minister to other Asian groups. One notable effort was to establish an Indian congregation for Tamil-speaking people. The Reverend S. Paul Theodore, from the Church of South India, was called by the consistory and installed by the classis as a missionary to Tamils on November 23, 1986. The congregation flourished until the untimely death of Pastor Theodore. Later, this congregation left Newtown and affiliated with the United Church of Christ.

The Classis of Queens extended its welcome to another Taiwanese church when it approved the use of the former Second Reformed Church of Astoria by the Union Taiwanese Church. Although another denomination offered the classis a handsome sum for the church building, the classis decided to use the structure to establish the Union Taiwanese Church. This church was organized January 8, 1984, with the Reverend Chung-Sheng Lin as pastor.

The growth of Taiwanese churches in the RCA is quite remarkable. There are now nine organized churches in the New York Area, seven in New York, and two in New Jersey. This number becomes even more significant when it is pointed out that only two Taiwanese churches in the New York area are not affiliated with the Reformed Church in America. One is United Methodist and one is Presbyterian. It is as if the word is out in the Taiwanese community that if you want to affiliate with best church in America, come to the RCA.

The way the Reformed Church welcomed a young student named John Chang can serve as an example of a wider spirit of welcome. John came to the United States to pursue his theological training at Princeton Theological Seminary. While he was a student, he was invited to serve a new independent Taiwanese congregation on Staten Island. As he anticipated graduation, the congregation invited him to stay in the United States and serve them as their minister. In seeking to do this, John contacted the Presbyterian Church for help but was told that they could not receive him as a ministerial candidate and that he would have to return to Taiwan for ministry.

When he approached the Reformed Church, he found a willingness to sit down and try to help him and the new congregation. First of all, he was welcomed into the membership of the Reformed Church in Staten Island. That church affirmed his ministry to the Taiwanese congregation by electing him elder and then charging him to provide spiritual care to the Taiwanese group on the consistory's behalf, thereby becoming a full partner in ministry with him. He also enrolled at New Brunswick Theological Seminary to qualify himself for ordination in the RCA. After the training and time requirements were met, the Classis of New York ordained him May 5, 1985 and subsequently organized the church he served as the Grace Christian Reformed Church.

This church built its own structure in 1992. The groundbreaking was November 22 of that year. The rain on that Sunday afternoon did not stop the schedule. On the contrary, the pastor, John Chang, described it this way: "The rain was the shower of blessing from God to soften the ground for us to dig easily."

John Chang has made most significant contributions to the Reformed Church. The Grace Christian Reformed Church has become a strong, multicultural congregation, with a powerful ministry among Caucasian families. In fact, this dynamic church recently added an English-speaking minister just for this ministry. In addition, Chang makes excellent contributions to the leadership of the RCA. He served as president of the Classis of New York and of the Synod of New York and serves ably on other boards and agencies of the church.

A Sad Experience

While there was a growing perception among Taiwanese that the Reformed Church gave a cordial welcome to Taiwanese pastors and churches, that perception was seriously challenged in the case of one church and its pastor who sought to be received into the membership of the Reformed Church.

In 1987, the Reverend Thomas Kao and the newly forming Kalam Taiwanese congregation sought to be received by the Classis of Brooklyn and to obtain the use of the former Woodlawn Reformed Church. Initial meetings went well. The classis and the church leaders developed a cordial relationship. Kao sent a letter of request for membership in the classis in June of 1987, and an outline of procedures to be followed were sent to by the classis in a letter in September of 1987. The letter suggested a target date in February 1988 for possible action of the Brooklyn Classis to receive the Kalam congregation.

The congregation began using the Woodlawn building and agreed to pay rental fees of $1,500 per month. It was their fond hope that the classis would allow them to continue to use the structure, and so they began to make modest repairs to the aging building. Meanwhile, the Woodlawn Committee of the classis began to explore other alternatives for the property. When the Kalam leaders heard that they might be asked to leave the Woodlawn building, they were greatly disillusioned. Subsequently, trust between the new church and the classis deteriorated and plans for its organization were delayed.

The Woodlawn committee estimated that the Woodlawn building was worth over a million dollars and was, therefore, a valuable asset of the classis. The committee then suggested to the Kalam people that they share facilities with another congregation until they could accumulate funds to buy their own building. Kao reported that the proposed facilities were too crowded and asked again that he and his people be permitted to stay at Woodlawn.

The RCA's Council for Pacific and Asian-American Ministries was clearly in anguish at the turn of events. On June 22, 1988, its executive committee wrote to the stated clerk of the Brooklyn Classis.

> The members of the Council for Pacific and Asian Ministries, meeting in full session of June 11, 1988, have asked us to communicate its concern regarding the Kalam Church, and implore you to reevaluate your decision to pursue this discussion of the sale of this property. We deeply feel that the people who wanted to belong were made to feel unwelcome. Our denominational theme of "A People Who Belong" has been overpowered by mammon.[7]

The classis executive committee responded to the letter, indicating that "if they (Kalam Church) expected to be given the use of the Woodlawn Reformed Church property in perpetuity without any significant equity investment on their part...it is not possible that discussions could have continued."[8] Later, the Kalam Church decided to take matters into their own hands, and, without formal notice, decided to leave Woodlawn. They found a welcome with the United Methodist Church and quietly went their way. This is one of the two Taiwanese churches in the New York-New Jersey region that are not Reformed. The other one is a Presbyterian congregation in New Jersey. The classis of Brooklyn had a host of issues to deal with and in no way should be characterized as inhospitable. Its commitment to new churches is clear. Only, as the classis committee patiently went about looking at all its options for the valuable Woodlawn building, it was perceived by Kalam to be saying that his congregation was not welcome.

But the attraction of Taiwanese people to the Reformed Church continued. In 1987, even though the RCA has never had a church

---

[7] Letter from the Council for Pacific and Asian-American Ministries, RCA, to the executive committee of the Classis of Brooklyn, June 11, 1988.

[8] Letter from the executive eommittee, Classis of Brooklyn, to the Council of Pacific and Asian-American Ministries, RCA, June 15, 1988.

in Boston, a newly formed church, the Boston Taiwanese Christian Church, contacted the Synod of New York through the Reverend Bill Lee, asking for information on how to affiliate. On January 1, 1988, the congregation voted to ask the Classis of Queens to organize the church, which was done July 10 under the leadership of the Reverend Phillip Lin, a Presbyterian pastor.

Why Queens and not the closest classis, which would have been Mid-Hudson? The pastor insisted that it was easier for he and his elder to attend meetings in Queens because it was the location of the LaGuardia Airport! They also noted that they would enjoy the fellowship of other Taiwanese pastors and elders in a classis that already had several Taiwanese churches. And they noted that Bill Lee, a member of Queens Classis, was the one who encouraged them to contact the RCA.

Other Taiwanese Reformed churches include:

1. A Taiwanese church at the Flushing Bowne Street Church was started in 1987 and organized May 12, 1991, with the Reverend Norman Chang as its pastor. It later merged with the Bowne Street Church.
2. The Formosan Reformed Church of Long Island was established September 29, 1985.
3. The Trinity Reformed Taiwanese Church was organized in 1990, in the facility of the Trinity Reformed Church in Ridgewood, Queens, under the leadership of the Reverend Burton Chen. Subsequently, this congregation moved to the Rockland-Westchester Classis and is now located at the Greenville Community (Reformed) Church in Scarsdale.

The Korean Church

Perhaps all immigrants yearn to be with other people of their own national origin and go to great lengths to locate where they can keep in touch with their culture and language. However, this effort seems more deliberate and conscious for Koreans than for those of other nationalities. Sometimes Koreans live in the United States for decades without learning enough English to go shopping comfortably in an English-speaking store.

Therefore, every Korean institution, especially the Korean church, becomes a most valued place for Korean people. First of all, Koreans are attracted to Christianity. Although Korea as a nation was only willing to receive missionaries late in the nineteenth century, Koreans have become ardent followers of the faith. Among the sights that greet a visitor to Seoul, or any other large city in Korea, are the huge numbers of crosses that are seen above structures of every sort, identifying them as churches.

In most Asian countries, Christians are a small minority, but in Korea more than twenty-five percent are Christian. In the United States, the percentage of immigrants coming into the church is even larger. They come for worship, they also come for culture and language, and they come for practical help. Pastors are magnets in the Korean community as people of great resources. The pastor is not only the spiritual advisor but also the one immigrants turn to for housing arrangements, educational information, immigration information, and job seeking. The pastor that is able to provide assistance in these areas becomes known in the Korean "grapevine," and his church will surely grow, from the contacts he makes and the help he provides.

Korean pastors are hard working and devout. Sometimes they will keep cots in their offices so that they can stay there all night, spending long hours in prayer before catching a little sleep. Many Korean pastors conduct morning services Monday through Saturday at 6 a.m., even if the attendance is small. In the larger churches there will be two or more early morning services, some as early as 5 a.m., to accommodate workers who want to stop at the church for worship before going to work.

The Korean Reformed Churches

As noted above, the first Korean church to be organized in the East Coast synods was the Korean Philippo Reformed Church. The

Philippo congregation had come to the RCA by using the building of the former First Reformed Church of Long Island City. Its location, not far from the East River, was set among the farms of Long Island at its founding in 1874, but it had seen its surroundings change dramatically over the years. By 1979, when the church was officially disbanded, the neighborhood had become industrial in character and only a few feet from an elevated train that rumbles by every few minutes. The congregation had been in decline for many years, with the last pastor, the Reverend LeRoy Suess, leaving in 1965.

Nevertheless, the Korean Philippo Church was organized there in 1979 and flourished. Attending the organization service was one of the first acts that I did after I arrived as the new synod executive that year. It was the first church to be organized as an Asian congregation since the Japanese United Church was organized in 1949.

The Shin Kwang Reformed Church

No story of the Asian Reformed churches should leave out the Shin Kwang Church of Bayside, Queens. The man with the vision there was the Reverend Jae Hong Han. Han was a graduate of Hope College and New Brunswick Theological Seminary, was ordained by the Central California Classis in 1978, and established the Korean Reformed Presbyterian Church in San Francisco in 1982. In that year, he came to Queens to serve a large Presbyterian Korean church in Flushing, Queens. Leaving that church, he came to the Queens Classis and asked if he could gather a congregation under its auspices. He proceeded with the development of a new church and obtained the use of the Vocational Training School in Astoria, Queens.

The facilities provided for the worshipers were inadequate and there was considerable prejudice against them, but they persevered and grew to a congregation of about two hundred members, which was organized by the classis in 1988. The church then launched a concerted effort to find a building site. It finally found one large enough, about one acre, with a house at one end that was to serve as a parsonage, in Bayside, Queens. The only problem was its cost: $1,450,000. Even though the church had garnered $500,000 in gifts and pledges, the financial need was huge, especially for a new church, and especially because the purchase was basically for land.[9]

Usually, Reformed Church building loans are made for construction, not land purchase. In 1988, the Church Planning and Development Division of the General Program Council, after considerable debate, finally agreed to loan the church $1,000,000 so that the site could be purchased. It was the largest loan ever made to a Reformed church up to that time. A stipulation was added, however, that no construction was to begin until the loan was repaid, a stipulation that caused considerable anguish and controversy.

But the people at Shin Kwang were eager to start building. They wanted to move to the bricks and mortar stage, not to spend five or ten years or more in a broken-down school facility where they were not wanted while they paid off a loan which would not build their dream. The church they designed was magnificent; it was to have a sanctuary that would seat five hundred, a gymnasium, and a school. And they were eager to start building, so they did! They used gifts from the offering plate designated for construction to proceed. The church leaders claimed they did not understand the stipulation not to build and that they would keep up with payments on the loan and only use cash for construction.

Now what was the Reformed Church to do? Foreclose? Of course not, even though there was serious discussion about doing it. Some predicted that, eventually, the project would fail and that the denomination would be left with great debts. Complicating matters further was the fact that the church's classis assessment payments were always behind and accompanied by statements from Han that assessments were simply too high.

---

9   From files of the Regional Synod of New York, Tarrytown, New York.

Eventually the building was built with cash contributions and gerry-built temporary financing. It was dedicated October 3, 1992. However, not until 1999 was refinancing arranged that satisfied the requirements of the Reformed Church. Against all odds, this church and its ministry was finally built. Shin Kwang, while being built amidst criticism, is nonetheless one of the fastest growing churches in the Queens Classis. Jae Han, still its pastor, is a dynamic preacher and a man of great energy; his gifts were used to build one of the strongest Korean churches in the RCA.

Koreans in the Bronx

At the same time Koreans were moving into other parts of the city of New York. In the Bronx, for instance large numbers of Koreans were taking up residence, working hard to establish themselves, mostly by setting up small businesses such as dry cleaners, fruit stores, nail salons, or gift shops. Those who could not raise the capital for their own shops would usually work for another Korean who had set up a business.

One pastor, now a most honored leader in the Korean Reformed Church, is the Reverend Eun Soo Lee. At the suggestion of the Reverend John Pyo Lee, he knocked on the door of the offices of the Synod of New York and asked for help in locating a place for his new congregation in the Bronx. Lee had a small congregation, the Dong San Church, of around fifty people, but he had large dreams of what the Lord was going to do with his congregation.

He wanted a site where it would be possible to establish a school as well as a church. Together, we went looking, mostly at commercial buildings that had the potential of being converted to church and school use. The ones he wanted to purchase were all too expensive for his small church, so he expressed an interest in working with an under-utilized Reformed church that would be willing to take in the congregation.

After several contacts, the Bronx Williamsbridge Road Reformed Church was selected for discussion. The minister at that time was the Reverend Alan Koller, who was serving as stated supply and teaching at Fordham University. The meeting with the consistory went well. When members of the consistory heard that the Dong San Church wanted to become a Reformed church and would assume all the expenses related to the upkeep of the building, they agreed to allow the Dong San people to begin Sunday services, as well as a number of other activities in the building.

A close relationship developed. Dong San became an organized congregation February 8, 1981, the second Korean church in the fold of the eastern Reformed Church. The church grew in numbers and never lost its vision, nor did the pastor. In 1983, the congregation purchased the property next door, on which stood an old commercial building and a house. They removed the commercial building and made a parking lot and converted the residence into a church house for education and built a small chapel in the back.

So well did the relationship develop with the Williamsbridge Road Church that on January 22, 1989, the two congregations merged into the United Reformed Church of Williamsbridge Road and invited the Reverend Lynn Hanousek to be their English-speaking pastor.

But the dream kept on growing. A second site was purchased in Westchester County. A commercial building originally built for ten indoor tennis courts, on the top of a hill in Yonkers along the New York Thruway, was purchased for over a million dollars. The building had over 70,000 square feet of space. When completely converted, it will contain a church, a chapel, a school, a youth facility, a host of meeting rooms, and a recreation area and indoor parking. Much of this use is already in place. The Williamsbridge Road facility will be retained for additional ministry.

Other Korean Churches

The following churches are not mentioned above but have significant ministry in the Synod of New York:[10]

10 *MGS*, various years.

1. The Classis of Queens organized the Siloam Korean Reformed Church November 10, 1985. Its pastor is the Reverend Mon Soo Oh, who was succeeded by the Reverend Jong Duk Kim. Later, this congregation acquired its own building in Flushing.

2. The Nakwon Korean Church started at the Sunnyside Reformed Church, grew rapidly, then purchased and renovated a large former VFW building on Queens Boulevard, dedicating it October 11, 1992, with the Reverend Soo Sik Lim, pastor.

3. The Immanuel American Korean Church was a deliberate church start of the Queens Classis. The Reverend Suk Hong Song was called as the organizing pastor November 17, 1986. The church was organized in 1986, but after the pastor left for another field, problems arose. The congregation changed its name to the Emmaus Church and moved to the Whitestone Presbyterian Church. Shortly after that move, the church was dropped by the classis when it left the RCA.

4. The Chuk Bok Presbyterian (Reformed) in Flushing was organized Sunday, October 25, 1992, using the facilities of the Trinity Lutheran Church building. The pastor was Byung Ho Ahn. The church was later disbanded when its small membership could no longer sustain itself.

5. The Chiyang Korean Church was provided the use of the building of the former Ridgewood Reformed Church. The church was organized June 1, 1986, and the pastor, the Reverend Chang Whan Kim, was installed.

6. The Choongsyn Korean Church started at the Steinway Reformed Church, before moving to its own building. It was organized by the Classis of Queens in 1996. The pastor is the Reverend John Y. Hahn.

7. The Roslyn Heights New Church of Greater New York has come to membership in the RCA from the Presbyterian

Church, USA. The Classis of Nassau-Suffolk organized this large church in 1996. The Reverend Hak Qwon Lee is the pastor. It was in this church where the first ordination of a Korean woman in the synods of New York or Mid-Atlantics took place. The Reverend Young Na is a graduate of New Brunswick Seminary. The only other ordained Korean woman in the Synod of New York is the Reverend Esther H. Min, a minister at the Shin Kwang Church in Queens, who transferred to the classis from the Korean Presbyterian Church in 1987.

The Chinese Church

Although most of the people in RCA Taiwanese churches are of Chinese heritage, it is important that the distinctions between them and Chinese from the mainland be understood. Presently, there is one Chinese church in the New York Synod, the Chinese Community (Reformed) Church, a tenant congregation of the Presbyterian church on 96th Street and Central Park West in Manhattan in New York City. The Reverend Carpus Yip became pastor September 20, 1987. The Reverend Laura Lin, a daughter of the church and a graduate of New Brunswick Seminary, was ordained at the same service. She became its pastor March 29, 1992. This is one of two Chinese churches that joined the RCA in 1984, under the leadership of the Reverend Phillip Lee.

The other was the Chinese Community Church, which was welcomed by the First Reformed Church, Hastings-on-Hudson, to use their chapel. The Hastings Chinese Church had a great difficulty finding a suitable new minister after Lee left to return to Hong Kong in 1984. Eventually, this church asked the Classis of Rockland-Westchester to be dropped from membership to become an independent church. They subsequently called a Baptist pastor to serve them. The congregation still uses the Hastings Chapel as a tenant and maintains a good relationship with them.

Lee also sought to help establish a Chinese church in Yonkers, using the former Lincoln Park building. Through his efforts and contacts, a congregation of ethnic Chinese people from Thailand was formed and organized by the Classis of Rockland-Westchester. The Reverend Santi Phattanachitchhon was the founding pastor.

Factors That Make the RCA an Attractive Choice for Asians

Why is it that the RCA's Synod of New York is in the center of activity in developing new Asian churches? Looking at other denominations reveals that our growth, proportionately, outstrips their growth of Asian populations. This calls for some conjecture, which I offer, as one who has listened to Korean, Taiwanese, and other Asians for more than twenty years. Here is what I conclude:

1. The Reformed Church is well thought of by its overseas church partners and, therefore, by the pastors who come to the United States. In the case of Taiwan, we have long sent missionaries who are highly respected. Their work and their commitment to Jesus Christ have brought high regard to the Reformed Church. As for Korea, where we have never sent missionaries, it is well known that the first Presbyterian missionary, Horace G. Underwood, was a graduate of New Brunswick Seminary. Deep respect for him brings high regard to the church of his training and ordination.

2. The Reformed Church is also well regarded in China and Japan, where we have had a long, fruitful missionary presence. Where there would be a concentration of immigration from these nations, I believe we would also have a great opportunity for church growth.

3. The Reformed Church is known in among Asians as a biblical church with strong fundamental values. Further, it has a reputation for being somewhat more conservative theologically and socially than our Presbyterian compatriots,

and more in line with the attitudes held by Christians in Taiwan and Korea.

4. The Reformed Church has a joint mission with the Presbyterians in Taiwan and Japan and a partnership with the Korean Presbyterian Church in Korea. There we are regarded as Presbyterians as well as Reformed, so there is no brand name problem with pastors coming from these nations.

5. The Synod of New York has a reputation for giving a welcome to immigrants. Over the years, the synod has looked for ways to help new congregations and pastors. This has meant finding buildings and finances. The synod is perceived as part of a church that reaches out with a welcome to new pastors and congregations and has been willing to be creative in solving problems, including those posed by the *Book of Church Order*.

The Future of the Asian Church and the RCA

In each case, these new churches will face two crises. The first will come when the immigration patterns from Asia stop or slow and the ready supply of new members is no longer available. The second crisis will come when the first generation ages and dies, and their Asian language is supplemented or perhaps supplanted by English. The new congregations are growing largely because of the arrival of immigrants from their homelands.

This crisis will face each of the Asian church groups differently. The Japanese, for instance, have never had large numbers of immigrants and, hence, have not experienced rapid growth. The Japanese church in New York has a steady membership and, with a history going back several generations, has accommodated itself to a mixture of Japanese and English in its worship and church life. Nearly everyone is bilingual, but the service is led in Japanese for the few who do not understand English and as a mark of the congregation's love for its original language.

The Korean church is still so new to the American scene that language and culture are major hallmarks of every church. It also appears that Koreans strive to continue their lives in a Korean context whenever possible. They have, thus far, not integrated into English-speaking churches, but have a preference for things Korean. This is seen with the appearance of large numbers of Korean shops and businesses where there is a concentration of Koreans in a section of New York. Parts of Flushing, Queens, have such a profusion of Korean shops and signs that they look like a suburb of Seoul.

There is no rush to use English in the Reformed Asian churches. Most strive to keep not only their language but also their cultural styles. The latter is seen in the way the Reformed Church's liturgical and polity standards are adapted in Asian, especially in the Korean churches. The offices of elder and deacon, for example, are viewed and presented in quite different ways from a standard Reformed church. Koreans traditionally believe that the average church member cannot qualify for these two offices. Only after years of service can an individual—and it is usually a man—be qualified as a deacon. An elder can be chosen only after years of faithful service as a deacon and exemplary spiritual leadership that is affirmed universally by the members of his congregation. This means that the organization of a new Korean church will often be delayed for several years. The first step will be to train a cadre of leaders who are referred to as "temporary deacons" but not ordained. From this group of ten to forty, one or two will be selected for ordination as deacons and, finally, one who demonstrates spiritual and leadership maturity will be set aside as an elder, at which time a consistory will be established. Typically, this means that at its organization, a church will have a hundred members, a consistory of three or four, and strong finances. There will also a full-time minister and one or two part-time student or assistant pastors. The latter will usually be in charge of the children's church and youth church, which will most likely meet at the same time as the main worship service.

The Korean church also recognizes the office of Qwanza. This is a nonordained office in which women may serve. This office is especially prized by Korean churches as a way to gather leadership from women who are traditionally barred from the office of deacon or elder. The Reformed Church, of course, does not know what to do with this office, which is so clearly unconstitutional, so those who hear about it generally ignore it.

No one knows when immigration patterns from Asia will abate, though there are signs that it is slowing. When it happens, the Asian church will be confronted with much the same need to change as faced the Dutch when everything around them changed and the society they lived in became English-speaking. Even if immigration continues, all of these new churches will be faced with the death of the first generation and the ascendancy of the next generation, which will be English-speaking and probably more oriented to American culture.

Today, in the Asian church, there is great concern with this eventuality. Pastors are responding with alarm to the fact that the children of the first generation have lost the language of their parents and are becoming Americanized. This in-between generation is referred to as the "1.5" generation. The fears of the immigrant pastors are that, as the younger generation loses the ability to speak its Asian language, it will also leave the culture and may no longer identify with the Asian church. As an effort to head off this development, nearly every church has a Saturday language school for the children to retain or possibly relearn the tongue of their parents.

Some churches are addressing this concern with creative actions. The Reformed Church of Closter, New Jersey, one of the new Korean churches in the Synod of Mid-Atlantics, across the Hudson River from New York, carries out a cross-cultural ministry, in which Korean and English-speaking people share all aspects of church, including a bilingual Sunday morning worship service. This happens to be the church where I presently serve as copastor. The target for this ministry is the next generation of Koreans, who will be English speakers. The approach is unique among Korean-speaking churches, but may become a model of the future.

Another church that is developing a church for the future is the Asian American Church, which meets in a Baptist church in Syosset. The congregation started under the auspices of the Classis of Nassau-Suffolk in 1993, it was but not organized into a church. Its pastor is the Reverend Wai C. Tan. Services are in English but the members are of Japanese, Korean, Chinese, and other national backgrounds. As a congregation, though, growth has been slow; the ministry has typically appealed to young adults and has not built a sustainable community. Such visionary efforts are few today but may be expanded in the future.

It is clear that there is a dynamic place for the Asian church in the Reformed Church. Its people and pastors bring energy, commitment, and determination to build the Church of Jesus Christ. They are showing us what the call of God is all about. We have great cause to celebrate the Asian people and churches that have come join to the RCA as full partners of the gospel. And our opportunity to welcome them remains bright and promising.

Appendix A

A Pictorial View of
the Synod of New York
Russell L. Gasero

The following images offer only a brief visual glance at the ministry of the Regional Synod of New York. From the planting of the first Reformed congregation in New Netherland to the present day, the New York Synod has been a diverse and challenging region. These pictures relate to the essays presented in this volume and offer a sampling of the problems and prospects that are confronted in the Synod of New York.

Early street map of New Amsterdam

151

The Bushwick church in Brooklyn during the colonial period.

John Henry Livingston (1746-1825), the "Father of the Reformed Church in America," was the first General Synod professor of theology in 1784.

William Linn (1752-1808), a minister of the Collegiate Church, was appointed the first chaplain of the House of Representatives on May 1, 1789.

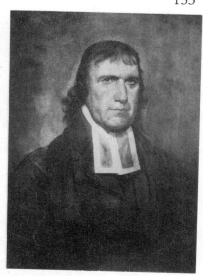

The Steinway Reformed Church, Astoria, New York, was organized for German immigrants by members of the Steinway family. It now houses three congregations worshiping in English, Greek, and Korean.

Harlem, New York
City, the home of the
East Harlem Protestant
Parish.

Urban Ministry

Elder Clyde Watts of the
Elmendorf Reformed Church,
New York City.

Rev. Don De Young outside
the Elmendorf church (below).

The Synod of New York has the longest continuing urban ministry in America. Here the Marble Collegiate Church stands against the Empire State Building in New York City.

Below, the church on St. Thomas, Virgin Islands, is a part of the Synod of New York. The congregation was established in 1660 and received from the Classis of Amsterdam in 1827.

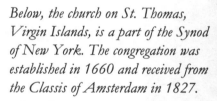

Newtown Reformed Church in Elmhurst, New York. The church was organized in 1731 and is now a joint English/Asian congregation.

A Diverse Membership

Communal meals have provided opportunities for fellowship for diverse groups of Christians since the New Testament period.

Mrs. Odu's primary
class at the Japanese
Christian Institute,
ca. 1933.

Rev. Giichi Kawamata (1888-
1959),ordained in Japan, was pastor
of the Japanese Christian Association
from 1930 to 1949 and the Japanese
American Church of Christ in New
York City from 1949 to 1959.

Rev. Boanerges Gomez
leads a Sunday School
class at The Elmendorf
Reformed Church in
New York City.

M. William Howard served as executive secretary of the RCA's Black Council/African American Council and as president of the National Council of Churches. He is now president of New York Theological Seminary.

The Reverend Wilbur T. Washington was in 1992 the first African American to be elected president of the General Synod. He also served as a professor at Central College and New Brunswick Theological Seminary, concluding his ministry at the First Reformed Church in Jamaica, Queens, New York.

Appendix B

A Chronological List of Congregations in the Synod of New York

Russell L. Gasero

Following is a list of congregations that have existed within the varying boundaries of the Synod of New York. James Brumm illustrates in his essay the moving of classes and congregations between the synods of Albany and New York. As the church moved westward, synods of Chicago, Iowa, and Michigan were established. Prior to their establishment, all congregations fell within the bounds of either the synod of New York or Albany.

Also included within the synod were the congregations of the Classis of Arcot, India. While this classis was a part of the synod, it was properly a mission field and is not reflected in this list. The list does include congregations established before the synod was organized in 1800 but which were still in existence at that time. The synod has nurtured more than five hundred congregations.

I have also attempted to include those congregations that were in the classes that moved back and forth between the synods of New York and Albany. The lines are often vague for those congregations which only lived for a few short years. Every attempt has been made to include all the congregations. My apologies for any that may have been omitted inadvertently.

1628

New York, NY - Collegiate Dutch Reformed

New York, NY - Mill Loft (disbanded)

1633

New York, NY - Frame Building (disbanded)

1642

New York, NY - Fort Amsterdam (disbanded)

1654

Brooklyn, NY - Bushwick (disbanded - 1919)

Brooklyn, NY - Flatbush Dutch

Brooklyn, NY - Flatlands

Kings Co., NY - Collegiate (disbanded - 1808)

1655

Brooklyn, NY - Gravesend

1659

Kingston, NY - First

1660

Brooklyn, NY - First

Jersey City, NJ - Old Bergen

New York, NY - Harlem (continued - 1886)

New York, NY - Stuyvesant's Chapel (disbanded)

St. Thomas, VI - St. Thomas

1663

New York, NY - Garden St (sp - 1812)

Staten Island, NY - Fresh Kills (merged - 1714)

1665

Staten Island, NY - South Side (merged - 1714)

1677

Brooklyn, NY - New Utrecht

1680

Staten Island, NY - Staten Island

1682

Hackensack, NJ - French (disbanded - 16??)

1683

New Paltz, NY - New Paltz

1686

Hackensack, NJ - Church on the Green, First

1688

New York, NY - French (transferred - 1804)

1693

Passaic, NJ - Old First

1694

Tappan, NY - Tappan

1696

Bronx, NY - Fordham Manor

1697

Belleville, NJ - Belleville

Tarrytown, NY - First (merged - 1990)

1699

Holmdel, NJ - Holmdel (merged - 1968)

Marlboro, NJ - Old Brick

Somerville, NJ - Raritan, First (merged - 1974)

1701

Accord, NY - Rochester

1702

Jamaica, NY - First

1703

Three Mile Run, NJ - Three Mile Run (dropped - 1754)

1710

Churchville, PA - North and Southampton

Franklin Park, NJ - Six Mile Run

Oakland, NJ - Ponds

Saugerties, NY - Saugerties

1714

Staten Island, NY - Richmond (dropped - 1777)

1715

Rhinebeck, NY - German (transferred - 1840)

1716

Fishkill, NY - First

Poughkeepsie, NY - Poughkeepsie

1717

Montrose, NY - Cortlandtown

New Brunswick, NJ - First

1719

Readington, NJ - Readington

1720

Fairfield, NJ - Fairfield

1722

Livingston, NY - Linlithgo

1724

Dumont, NJ - Old North

Schraalenburgh, NJ - Schraalenburgh (transferred - 1822)

1725

Ridgewood, NJ - Old Paramus

1726

Claverack, NY - Reformed Dutch

1727

Belle Mead, NJ - Harlingen

1728

Germantown, NY - Germantown

1729

New York, NY - Nassau Street (disbanded - 1844)

1731

Elmhurst, NY - First Newtown

Rhinebeck, NY - Rhinebeck

1732

Brookville, NY - Brookville

Manhasset, NY - Community

Montgomery, NY - Brick

1736

Pompton Plains, NJ - First

Wallkill, NY - Shawangunk

1737

Bushkill, PA - Bushkill

Montague, NJ - Minisink

Port Jervis, NY - Deepark

1738

Stone Ridge, NY - Marbletown

1741

Napanoch, NY - Warwarsing (dropped - 1964)

1744

St. Croix, VI - St. Croix (disbanded)

1746

Pine Plains, NY - Gallatin

1747

Lebanon, NJ - Lebanon

1749

West Nyack, NY - Clarkstown

1750

Warwick, NY - Warwick

1752

Neshanic, NJ - Neshanic

New Paltz, NY - Second (merged - 1778)

1755

Montville, NJ - Montville

Paterson, NJ - Totowa First (merged - 1927)

1757

Hopewell Junction, NY - Hopewell

1758

Bedminister, NJ - Bedminister

New York, NY - East 68th St (disbanded - 1968)

Wappingers Falls, NY - New Hope

1760

Hardwick, NJ - Hardwick (dropped - 1816)

1766

Millstone, NJ - Hillsborough

Red Hook Landing, NY - Old Red Hook (dropped - 1843)

1769

New York, NY - North (disbanded - 1875)

1770

Kingston, NY - German (dropped - 1783)

Ridgefield, NJ - English Neighborhood

Wallkill, NY - New Hurley

1774

Spring Valley, NY - West New Hempstead

1784

Upper Saddle River, NJ - Saddle River

1785

Mahwah, NJ - Ramapo

1787

Knowlton, NJ - Knowlton (transferred - 1805)

1788

Clove, NJ - Clove (transferred - 1818)

Red Hook, NY - St. Johns

1790

Elmsford, NY - Elmsford

1791

Shokan, NY - Shokan

Ulster Park, NY - Ulster Park (disbanded - 1965)

1792

Hyde Park, NY - Hyde Park

White House Station, NJ - Rockaway

1796

Bloomington, NY - Bloomington (merged - 1969)

1797

Almond, NY - Karr Valley (disbanded - 1819)

Sharon, PA - Sharon (dropped - 1819)

Tuscarora, PA - Tuscarora (dropped - 1830)

1799

Peekskill, NY - Peekskill (merged - 1834)

1801

Bloomfield, NJ - Brookdale

Hurley, NY - Hurley

1802

Wayne, NJ - Preakness

Woodbourne, NY - Woodbourne

1803

New York, NY - Greenwich (disbanded - 1868)

1805

New York, NY - Bloomingdale (disbanded - 1913)

1805

Woodstock, NY - Dutch

Wurtsboro, NY - Wurtsboro

1806

Willow Grove, PA - Philadelphia - First

Wyckoff, NJ - Wyckoff

1807

High Falls, NY - Clove (merged - 1958)

New York, NY - Second Garden Street (disbanded - 1812)

Saugerties, NY - Flatbush

1808

New York, NY - Madison Avenue (disbanded - 1918)

Staten Island, NY - Richmond (disbanded - 1886)

1812

New York, NY - South (disbanded - 1914)

Park Ridge, NJ - Pascack

Pompton Lakes, NJ - Pompton

1815

Pine Bush, NY - New Prospect

1816

Pleasant Plains, NY - Pleasant Plains (transferred - 1823)

1817

New York, NY - Market St (disbanded - 1869)

Philadelphia, PA - Second (disbanded - 1918)

1818

Philadelphia, PA - Second (transferred - 1820)

1819

Beacon, NY - Beacon

Berea, NY - Berea (dropped - 1902)

Bloomingburg, NY - Bloomingburg (merged - 1964)

1820

Hawthorne, NY - Hawthorne

Staten Island, NY - Brighton Heights

1821

Spotswood, NJ - Spotswood

1823

New York, NY - African (dropped
- 1829)

New York, NY - Seventh Ave
(merged - 1859)

New York, NY - Thirty-fourth St
(merged - 1896)

1824

Brooklyn, NY - New Lots

1825

Beekman, NY - Beekman (dropped
- 1831)

North Branch, NJ - North Branch

1826

New York, NY - Orchard St
(disbanded - 1832)

1827

Philadelphia, PA - Fourth (merged
- 1969)

Wyckoff, NJ - Second

1829

Bayonne, NJ - First Federated

Brooklyn, NY - Williamsburgh
(disbanded - 1941)

New York, NY - Manhattan
(disbanded - 1873)

New York, NY - Vandewater St
(disbanded - 1831)

1830

Jersey City, NJ - First (merged -
1886)

Pottsville, PA - Pottsville (dropped
- 1831)

1831

Dashville Falls, NY - Rifton Glen
(disbanded - 1923)

Marshallville, NY - Marshallville
(disbanded - 1839)

New York, NY - Ninth St (sp -
1855)

1832

Blawenburg, NJ - Blawenburg

1833

Flemington, NJ - Clover Hill

Libertyville, NY - Guilford (merged
- 1930)

New York, NY - North St
(disbanded - 1837)

Newark, NJ - First Hispanic

Stanton, NJ - Stanton

1834

Middlebush, NJ - Middlebush

Somerville, NJ - Raritan, Second
(merged - 1974)

1835

Hudson, NY - First

Newburgh, NY - Meadow Hill

1836

Hudson, NY - Mt. Pleasant

Long Island City, NY - First Astoria

Middletown, NJ - Middletown

New York, NY - St Paul's
(disbanded - 1877)

Philadelphia, PA - Roxborough
(transferred - 1854)

1837

Brooklyn, NY - Central (disbanded
- 1851)

Fairview, IL - Fairview

Glenham, NY - Glenham (merged - 1968)

Little Falls, NJ - First

New York, NY - Washington Square (disbanded - 1877)

Philadelphia, PA - Third (disbanded - 1891)

1838

Mellenville, NY - Mellenville (merged - 1968)

Mount Marion, NY - Plattekill

New York, NY - German Evang Mission (merged - 1911)

Nyack, NY - First

Walden, NY - First

1839

Bronx, NY - West Farms, First (disbanded - 1948)

Brooklyn, NY - East New York (merged - 1910)

Katsbaan, NY - Katsbaan

New York, NY - Collegiate Middle

Piermont, NY - First

Saugerties, NY - Katsbaan

1840

Brooklyn, NY - Fourth (disbanded - 1844)

Brooklyn, NY - South (merged - 1975)

Brunswick, IL - Copperas (transferred - 1849)

Ellenville, NY - Ellenville

Irvington, NJ - First (disbanded - 1989)

1841

Trenton, NJ - First (dropped - 1849)

Vanderveer, IL - Vanderveer (disbanded - 1869)

1842

Brooklyn, NY - North of Gowanus (merged - 1850)

Flushing, NY - Flushing (merged - 1974)

Freehold, NJ - Freehold

Princeton, NJ - Griggstown

Scarsdale, NY - Greenville Community

Yonkers, NY - First (merged - 1924)

1843

New Brunswick, NJ - Second

New York, NY - Stanton St (transferred - 1849)

New York, NY - Washington Heights (disbanded - 1868)

North Bergen, NJ - Grove

Pekin, IL - Pekin (transferred - 1914)

Rosendale, NY - Rosendale (merged - 1969)

1844

Grahamsville, NY - Grahamsville

1845

Port Washington, NJ - Port Washington (dropped - 1847)

1846

Brooklyn, NY - Middle (disbanded - 1887)

Jersey City, NJ - Wayne St (merged - 1923)

New York, NY - Mt Pleasant (disbanded - 1867)

South Bound Brook, NJ - Bound Brook

1847

Brooklyn, NY - Bedford (disbanded - 1904)

Keyport, NJ - Keyport

Poughkeepsie, NY - Second (merged - 1914)

Washington, IL - Washington (disbanded - 1855)

1848

Brooklyn, NY - Greenpoint

Claryville, NY - Claryville

Gladstone, NJ - Peapack

New York, NY - German Evang, Second (disbanded - 1865)

Newark, NJ - Second (merged - 1940)

Newark, NJ - Third (dropped - 1861)

Raritan, NJ - Third

South Holland, IL - First

West Hurley, NY - West Hurley (disbanded - 1947)

1849

Kingston, NY - Fair Street

Milwaukee, WI - New Life

South Holland, IL - Thorn Creek

Staten Island, NY - Huguenot Park

1850

Bronxville, NY - Bronxville

Brooklyn, NY - Twelfth Street (disbanded - 1968)

Hastings-on-Hudson, NY - First

Hoboken, NJ - First (merged - 1967)

New York, NY - West (merged - 1859)

Oostburg, WI - First

Peekskill, NY - Van Nest (disbanded - 1957)

South Branch, NJ - South Branch

1851

Bronx, NY - Mott Haven

Brooklyn, NY - Church on the Heights (merged - 1931)

Brooklyn, NY - North (merged - 1902)

Brooklyn, NY - South Bushwick

Brown Settlement, NY - Brown Settlement (dropped - 1854)

Easton, PA - Easton (transferred - 1893)

Frankllin, WI - Franklin (dropped - 1925)

German Valley, IL - Silver Creek

Krumville, NY - Krumville

Long Branch, NJ - First

New Brunswick, NJ - Third (dropped - 1912)

New York, NY - Livingston (merged - 1859)

Piermont, NY - Second (disbanded - 1854)

Port Ewen, NY - Port Ewen

Saugerties, NY - Blue Mountain

Staten Island, NY - Stapleton (transferred - 1868)

Stone Ridge, NY - North Marbletown

Tarrytown, NY - Second (merged - 1991)

1852

Brooklyn, NY - New Brooklyn

Jeffersonville, NY - Jeffersonville (dropped - 1866)

Jersey City, NJ - Third (disbanded - 1935)

New York, NY - German Evan, Third (merged - 1867)

1853

Berwyn, IL - First

Brooklyn, NY - German Evangelical (merged - 1919)

Burlington, IA - Burlington (dropped)

Jersey City, NJ - Hudson City (dropped - 1857)

Kerhonkson, NY - Federated

Mount Vernon, NY - First

New York, NY - Harlem German (transferred - 1862)

Union City, NJ - Christ (disbanded - 1980)

1854

Bayonne, NJ - Fifth St (merged - 1970)

Bronx, NY - Melrose Community (disbanded - 1984)

Brooklyn, NY - Bethesda Miss. (merged - 1869)

Cedar Grove, WI - First

Chicago, IL - Second (dropped - 1880)

Cuddebackville, NY - Cuddebackville

Long Island City, NY - Second Astoria (disbanded - 1982)

Manito, IL - Spring Lake (disbanded - 1931)

Mount Tremper, NY - Shandaken

New York, NY - German Evang, Fourth (disbanded - 1866)

New York, NY - Collegiate Marble

1855

Brooklyn, NY - Lee Ave. (merged - 1871)

Cold Spring, NY - Cold Spring (dropped - 1915)

East Millstone, NJ - East Millstone (disbanded - 1975)

Ellenville, NY - Second (dropped - 1862)

Elmhurst, NY - Newtown, Second (disbanded - 1942)

Hackensack, NJ - Second

Maspeth, LI, NY - East Williamsburgh (disbanded - 1912)

Nutley, NJ - Franklin

Raritan, IL - Raritan

Staten Island, NY - Tottenville (dropped - 1858)

Warren, NJ - Warren (transferred - 1870)

1856

Calicoon Center, NY - St. Paul's (merged - 1995)

Colts Neck, NJ - Colts Neck

Hoboken, NJ - German (merged - 1930)

Jersey City, NJ - Fourth (dropped -)

New York, NY - Central (disbanded - 1861)

Newark, NJ - North

Paterson, NJ - First Holland (disbanded - 1971)

1857

Metuchen, NJ - Metuchen

New York, NY - Seventh Ave (disbanded - 1859)

Rocky Hill, NJ - First

1858

Athens, PA - Athens (disbanded - 1878)

Hackensack, NJ - Third

Milesville, NY - Milesville (dropped - 1871)

New York, NY - Fourth German (dropped - 1925)

North Plainfield, NJ - First German (transferred - 1987)

Queens Village, NY - Queens

Woodhaven, LI, NY - Woodhaven (dropped - 1860)

1859

Brooklyn, NY - Bergen Hill (dropped - 1861)

Jersey City, NJ - Hudson City Second

Lodi, NJ - First (merged - 1967)

New York, NY - Union (disbanded - 1900)

1860

New York, NY - Prospect Hill (merged - 1910)

Staten Island, NY - Tompkinsville Second (disbanded - 1861)

1861

New York, NY - DeWitt Chapel (merged - 1895)

New York, NY - North Trinity (disbanded - 1862)

1862

Closter, NJ - Closter

Dingman's Ferry, PA - Walpack, Upper (disbanded - 1959)

Philadelphia, PA - Fifth (disbanded - 1967)

Philadelphia, PA - Fourth (dropped - 1867)

1863

Jersey City, NJ - Lafayette (merged - 1973)

Kingston, NY - Church of the Comforter

Plainfield, NJ - Central (dropped - 1880)

1864

Paterson, NJ - Broadway (merged - 1967)

Richboro, PA - Addisville

Saint Remy, NY - Saint Remy

1865

New York, NY - Harlem Lane (dropped)

Pottersville, NJ - Pottersville

Spring Valley, NY - Spring Valley (merged - 1980)

White Plains, NY - White Plains (dropped - 1874)

1866

Annandale, NJ - Annandale

Fort Lee, NJ - First of the Palisades

High Bridge, NJ - High Bridge

Millbrook, NY - Lyall Memorial

New York, NY - Holland (disbanded - 1897)

New York, NY - Knox (disbanded - 1944)

New York, NY - Manor (disbanded - 1956)

Newark, NJ - First German (disbanded - 1966)

Paterson, NJ - Main Street (disbanded - 1875)

West Sayville, NY - New Life

1867

North Haledon, NJ - Sixth

1868

Boonton, NJ - First

Brooklyn, NY - Myrtle Ave Miss (merged - 1869)

Jersey City, NJ - West End (dropped - 1878)

Newark, NJ - South (merged - 1926)

Passaic, NJ - Second (disbanded - 1922)

Philadelphia, PA - Bethune (disbanded - 1869)

1869

Brooklyn, NY - Bethany Chapel (merged - 1902)

New York, NY - North Church Chapel (disbanded - 1961)

New York, NY - Seventh Ave Chapel (separated - 1885)

Wallkill, NY - Wallkill

1870

Germantown, NY - Livingston Memorial

1871

Brooklyn, NY - Grace

Locust Valley, LI, NY - Locust Valley

North Branch, NY - North Branch (dropped - 1881)

1872

College Point, LI, NY - First

Jamaica, NY - St. Paul's (merged - 1958)

New York, NY - St Nicholas (disbanded - 1949)

1874

Bronx, NY - Union of Highbridge

Brooklyn, NY - Flatbush, Second (disbanded - 1965)

Jericho, LI, NY - Jericho (merged - 1877)

New York, NY - Avenue B (merged - 1919)

1875

Long Island City, NY - First (disbanded - 1979)

1876

Accord, NY - Lyonsville

Brooklyn, NY - Canarsie

Brooklyn, NY - Centennial Chapel
(dropped - 1893)

1878

Cherrytown, NY - Cherrytown
(dropped - 1879)

1879

Long Island City, NY - Steinway

1881

New York, NY - DeWitt

Staten Island, NY - Saint Peter's
German (dropped - 1918)

1883

Hicksville, LI, NY - First (merged -
1953)

1885

Brooklyn, NY - Ocean Hill
(disbanded - 1938)

New York, NY - Grace (disbanded
- 1921)

New York, NY - Yorkville German
(dropped - 1895)

Staten Island, NY - Port Richmond
(merged - 1905)

1886

New York, NY - Harlem Collegiate
(disbanded - 1911)

1887

New York, NY - Hamilton Grange
(merged - 1937)

Youngsville, NY - Youngsville
(merged - 1995)

1890

Gardiner, NY - Gardiner

New York, NY - Vermilye Chapel
(merged - 1935)

1891

Brooklyn, NY - Edgewood
(disbanded - 1964)

Brooklyn, NY - Greenwood Heights
(disbanded - 1972)

Glendale, NY - Glendale

Ridgewood, NY - Ridgewood
(merged - 1989)

Woodhaven, LI, NY - Grace
(dropped - 1894)

1892

New York, NY - Collegiate West
End

Yonkers, NY - Park Hill (merged -
1924)

1893

Bronx, NY - Anderson Memorial
of Belmont (disbanded - 1929)

New Hyde Park, NY - First

New York, NY - Bethany Memorial

1894

Bronx, NY - Comforter (disbanded
- 1976)

1895

Bronx, NY - University Heights
(dropped - 1900)

New York, NY - Thirty-fourth St
(disbanded - 1920)

New York Mills, NY - New York Mills (dropped - 1911)

1896

Brooklyn, NY - Bay Ridge (merged - 1918)

Long Island City, NY - Sunnyside

New York, NY - Sunshine Chapel (disbanded - 1938)

Port Jervis, NY - West End (merged - 1969)

1897

Brooklyn, NY - Emmanuel (disbanded - 1908)

Tillson, NY - Tillson (merged - 1969)

1898

Colonie, OK - Columbia Memorial (dropped - 1933)

1900

Brooklyn, NY - Woodlawn (disbanded - 1989)

Staten Island, NY - Prince Bay

Yonkers, NY - Mile Square (disbanded - 1974)

1901

Fort Sill, OK - Fort Sill (merged - 1913)

1902

Brooklyn, NY - Bethany (disbanded - 1919)

Cordell, OK - Cordell (transferred - 1911)

Harrison, OK - Harrison (dropped - 1909)

Liberty, OK - Liberty (dropped - 1909)

1903

Arapahoe, OK - Arapahoe (transferred - 1911)

New York, NY - Faith Mission (merged - 1928)

1904

Clinton, OK - Clinton (transferred - 1911)

1905

Staten Island, NY - Mariner's Harbor (disbanded - 1974)

1906

Gotebo, OK - Gotebo (transferred - 1911)

Moore, OK - Case Township (dropped - 1908)

Thomas, OK - Thomas (transferred - 1912)

1907

Lawton, OK - Commanche

Shawnee, OK - Horton Memorial (disbanded - 1911)

Woodside, NY - Winfield

1908

Oklahoma City, OK - Oklahoma City (disbanded - 1911)

Tulsa, OK - Tulsa (dropped - 1909)

1909

Far Rockaway, LI, NY - First (disbanded - 1973)

New York, NY - Collegiate Ft. Washington

1910

Brooklyn, NY - Barren Island
(disbanded - 1916)

Brooklyn, NY - Windsor Terrace
(disbanded - 1918)

Poughkeepsie, NY - Arlington

Woodhaven, NY - Forest Park

1911

Bronx, NY - Zion German
Evangelical (merged - 1944)

New York, NY - Harlem (disbanded
- 1950)

Peekskill, NY - Magyar (disbanded
- 1931)

Yonkers, NY - Crescent Place

1912

New York, NY - Harlem Elmendorf

Saugerties, NY - High Woods

1913

Hudson, NY - Hungarian
(disbanded - 1918)

Scarsdale, NY - Scarsdale (merged -
1921)

Valley Stream, LI, NY - Valley
Stream (dropped - 1918)

1914

Poughkeepsie, NY - Emmanuel
(dropped - 1931)

1915

Douglaston, NY - Community

Staten Island, NY - Clove Road
(disbanded - 1920)

1919

New York, NY - Waldensian
(dropped - 1921)

Ridgewood, NY - Trinity

1922

Newburgh, NY - Church of Our
Savior (disbanded - 1963)

Poughkeepsie, NY - Italian
(dropped - 1931)

1923

Bronx, NY - Church of the Master

1924

Yonkers, NY - Park Hill First
(transferred - 1964)

1925

Kew Gardens, NY - First

1926

Garden City Park, NY - Merillon
Neighborhood (? - 1987)

Yonkers, NY - Lincoln Park
Community

1927

Flushing, NY - Church on the Hill

Staten Island, NY - Charleston
(disbanded - 1971)

1929

Cambria Heights, NY - Community

Flushing, NY - Queensboro Hill

Hempstead, LI, NY - Hempstead
(disbanded - 1980)

Williston Park, NY - Williston Park

1932

Bronx, NY - West Farms Annex
(merged - 1936)

1936

Bronx, NY - Williamsbridge Road
(merged - 1989)

1938

Bayside, NY - Colonial

1940

Cottekill, NY - Cottekill (disbanded - 1976)

1941

Baldwin, LI, NY - Community (disbanded - 1974)

1949

Levittown, LI, NY - Community

New York, NY - Japanese American United

1951

Hicksville, NY - Parkway Community

1957

Plainview, LI, NY - Plainview

1960

North Babylon, NY - Saint Paul's

1962

High Falls, NY - Community

1963

Massapequa, LI, NY - Massapequa

1966

Stony Brook, NY - Christ Community

1969

Bloomington, NY - United of Rosendale

Woodside, NY - Winfield Taiwanese

1974

Flushing, NY - Bowne Street Community

1975

Brooklyn, NY - Bay Ridge United

1976

Brooklyn, NY - Christ Community

1977

Brooklyn, NY - New Life (disbanded - 1988)

New York, NY - Iglesia del Redentor (ca. 1977)

1979

Cary, NC - First

Long Island City, NY - Korean Philippo

1980

Elmhurst, NY - Newtown Taiwanese

Spring Valley, NY - United (merged)

1981

Bronx, NY - Korean Dong San (merged - 1989)

1983

Flushing, NY - Emmaus

1984

Hastings, NY - Chinese Community

Long Island City, NY - Taiwan Union

New York, NY - Chinese Community

1985

Long Island City, NY - Nakwon

Long Island City, NY - Siloam

New York, NY - Chinese Community (ca 1985)

Williston Park, NY - Formosan

1986

Hasting-on-Hudson, NY - Chinese Community (disbanded - 1986)

Ridgewood, NY - Chiuyang (merged - 1989)

1987

Flushing, NY - Bowne Street Taiwanese

1988

Flushing, NY - Shin Kwang

Framingham, MA - Boston Taiwanese

South Centerville, NY - Faith

1989

Bronx, NY - United of Williamsbridge Road (merged -)

Ridgewood, NY - Ridgewood (merged -)

1990

Ridgewood, NY - Trinity Christian Taiwanese

Staten Island, NY - Grace Christian

1991

Flushing, NY - Taiwanese American

Manorville, NY - Community

Tarrytown, NY - Reformed Church of the Tarrytowns

1992

Bayside, NY - Taiwanese American

Christiansted, St. Croix, VI - St. Croix

Flushing, NY - Chuk Bok (disbanded)

Long Island City, NY - Korean

Queens Village, NY - Iglesia De Cristo La Roca

1994

Yonkers, NY - Chour-Thai

1995

Youngsville, NY - United

1996

Flushing, NY - Chongsyn

Roslyn Heights, NY - New Church

Index

175